# CONIX ARCHITECTS

With contributions by Kas Oosterhuis & Moniek E. Bucquoye

stichting kunstboek

Guided by emotions,

inspired by beauty and creativity,

supported by experience, sustainability and context,

Conix Architects is continuously in motion.

Have you ever seen the movie *Independence Day*? A huge 15 mile wide spaceship hovering over Manhattan: an iconic image I will never forget. Floating buildings that seem to be suspended in air. When Ilona and I met Christine and Sylvie at the Atomium in Brussels, I had a similar experience: the nine bright spheres of the Atomium were hovering impressively over the new ticket office. From the counter you can see the spheres suspended in air, you are aware of the presence of the alien, as seen from the known and familiar. In the movie *Independence Day* the alien represents an evil force threatening life on earth, but here in Brussels the Atomium balls are like friendly aliens. The renovation, complete with the additional constructions and landscaping on ground level – all designed by Conix Architects – even adds to their friendly, communicative and inviting character.

Christine and Sylvie took us on a tour through the spheres; we travelled from ball to ball, through the tubes connecting the spheres. These sloping tubes are long stretched gates connecting and dividing, like the spokes of a space station, the nine spheres, which have now been developed into nine surprisingly different atmospheres. When visitors see the light grey construction in the interior of the spheres, they experience a feeling of absolute natural beauty and that's what first struck me too. The Conix interventions allow the visitor to appreciate the construction in its pure form. Unfortunately I did not go to the Expo in 1958 – regrettably my architect father did not take me with him, although I was almost nine years old at the time – but I think that the actual re-interpretation reveals the beauty of the original construction in a more effective way than the original itself. Conix succeeded in bringing forward an improved experience of the natural beauty of the 50-year-old masterpiece of the Belgium engineer André Waterkeyn.

Not unlike modern architects would approach the renovation of old landmark buildings from past eras, Conix Architects found a proper self-confident way to deal with the young Atomium monument. Their starting point was a respect for the existing construction, but they didn't declare it untouchable. They felt free to define their personal position with regard to this unique iconic structure and began to explore their own primary emotions in relation to the atomic configuration of the spheres. Before embarking on the actual design process, Conix Architects wanted to investigate their own emotional responses to this strong icon of progress and optimism of the late fifties. Only after getting it right in their heads, could they enclose the Atomium in their hearts. The emotional approach of this Antwerp based office convinced the client, who had – after a preliminary selection in the first round – also invited an architectural studio from Brussels to develop a proposal. Conix got the job and dealt with it successfully in every aspect: the urban approach of the Atomium, the landscaping in the shape of a folded lemniscate (symbol of infinity), the elegant ticket office set apart from the circular entrance of the Atomium itself, the dominant grey and white paint which propels forward the beauty of the structure and the choice for fifties design classics for the interior dressing. They also paid attention to the smallest delicate design interventions in the interior of each of the spheres in order to suit their new functions, namely a restaurant, congress facilities, exhibition spaces and even a sphere dedicated to children's play.

What can architects in general and Conix Architects in particular learn from the success of Atomium revisited? Re-interpretations of older structures are immensely popular with both their users and the general public. We were recently invited to Moscow, where we saw the magnificent Radio Tower of the brilliant engineer Shukov, whose work matches the structural boldness, architectural expression and above all the compassion of both the Eiffeltower and Waterkeyn's Atomium. What can we as architects, who design predominantly new structures without any relation to existing structures, learn from the Atomium case? To me it is obvious that the most successful renovations are indeed successful thanks to the presence of a strong engineering concept, which architects can cling to. But how should we design new-built structures then? Should we propose a strong engineering concept first and then re-interpret that concept ourselves as if it was designed in another era, belonging to another culture, or maybe even belonging to an alien civilisation? That would weave a stronger bond between architect and engineer indeed. The architectural/engineering [A / E] design team may act as both architect and engineer at the same time, supported by new software which allows the A / E designer to have immediate understanding of the behaviour and computation of complex structures. Maybe as A / E designers we could have improved the Atomium scheme itself. Maybe we could have found a better solution for the three emergency stairs, which now are oddly acting as support pylons for the tilted cubical formation of the nine spheres. They are almost destroying the experience of floating balls hanging out there, desperately longing for communication with our earth-bound civilisation.

Not only Conix Architects' intervention in the Atomium has made us aware of the potential of the renewed teaming up of architects and engineers, Conix Architects have also made an important step in the development of their own portfolio. Having established themselves convincingly as a leading Belgian modernist design studio, they are now being lured into the prospects of non-standard architecture which is dealing with the unique and the curvilinear complex. Making non-standard architecture is impossible without a strong, well-integrated A / E team, in which both parties give the best of their knowledge to develop new exciting and efficiently performing structures, which may eventually become the strong icons of the future and will be respected by future generations. Conix has learned from the fifties but at the same time proudly showed that the fifties can learn from today's architects as well. Writers, thinkers and designers are continuously rewriting and redesigning history by respecting, changing and adding to existing structures. Cities are dynamic factories with a sometimes vibrant celebration of life; no place on earth will ever be the same in its life-cycle. What today's architects can hope for is that future owners, users and re-interpreting architects will treat their buildings with respect by living, modifying and transforming them, and eventually by improving their A / E structures, placing them respectfully in the new context of future eras.

Principal ONL [Oosterhuis_Lénárd] bv

Vox + 31 10 2447039

Fax + 31 10 2447041

www.oosterhuis.nl

Professor Faculty of Architecture TU Delft

www.hyperbody.nl

Director Protospace Laboratory

www.protospace.bk.tudelft.nl

Client: ASBL Atomium vzw – Date: 2004 - 2006 – Area: 3.650 m² / 39.300 sq ft

## 001. ATOMIUM

COMPETITION - RENOVATION AND INTERIOR DESIGN - EXTENSION WITH NEW PAVILION AND URBAN DESIGN, BRUSSELS

During the competition, Conix Architects envisaged what it would be like for a visitor walking up from Boulevard du Centenaire to the Atomium for the first time, as if on a stage set. The boulevard had to be designed in such a way as to welcome visitors in a spectacular manner. The natural slope of the area was exploited to create a new approach, based on the infinite movement of the Moebius ring.

Groups of visitors can walk across the entire esplanade. A new pavilion has been added at the bottom of the Atomium, its inviting character enhancing the Atomium and giving it more flexibility because of the various relationships between the foot of the building, the esplanade and the position of the site, which includes Osseghem Park – the green lung of Expo '58. The existing roundabout will be transformed into a new, large square which offers visitors the opportunity to look at the Atomium from afar and from different angles. The new pavilion is the starting point of an artistic landscape tour through this landmark construction. The pavilion receives, orientates, links and sets the scene. It supports the functional aspect of the site through its commercial space, ticket office, sanitary and storage facilities. It adds an extra dimension to the Atomium as it is skillfully integrated into its surroundings through the use of materials such as satin stainless steel for the pavilion, which reflect the spheres of the Atomium.

The aim of this renovation project was to enhance and underline its contemporary ambitions. The renovated iron molecule is a shining example of how a new 'skin' has rejuvenated every sphere. This rejuvenation had to be reflected in the internal spaces as well, to bring back the Atomium's bygone charm. By studying the original documents and plans, Conix Architects pinpointed the purity of the spheres' design and recreated the atmosphere it had to evoke. This was done in the least intrusive way possible: covering the interior with galvanized steel and the exterior with stainless steel. Discovering the inner secrets of the Atomium becomes easier as you follow the blue stairs throughout the various spheres. The internal spaces of the Atomium flow uninterruptedly through one another via the spheres and tubes. The tubes act as emotional extensions of the structure. Conix Architects' emotional experience of the spheres is enhanced by the way they treated the interior. The light designer Ingo Maurer created lights especially for the Atomium which enhance the emotional atmosphere of the interior.

Six of the nine spheres are open to the public. The remaining three were never designed for public use and will remain empty. The glass volume surrounding the foot has been emptied and shops and other utilities have been moved to the pavilion. After buying your ticket in the pavilion, you start in the bottom sphere, which is dedicated to Expo '58. This signals the start of a journey of inspiration and emotion that created this structure and leads to the next sphere which houses temporary exhibitions. The next stop is the central sphere which boasts two bars, namely 'Stippenbar' and 'Bellenbar' where visitors can quench their thirst before taking the lift to the top sphere. The restaurant lounge offers magnificent views over the whole of Brussels. On the way down, you walk through the children's sphere, designed in conjunction with the artist Alicia Framis. This world of dreams is the gateway to a place where children can stay overnight in a mini-hotel, fully fitted with water molecules. Adults are only allowed to stand on the outside, looking into the magic world on their way out. Going down via the stairs, you approach the exit and the new square, where the visitors can relax on the new urban furniture or the new stairs integrated into the square and enjoy the Atomium's splendor from a different angle.

015

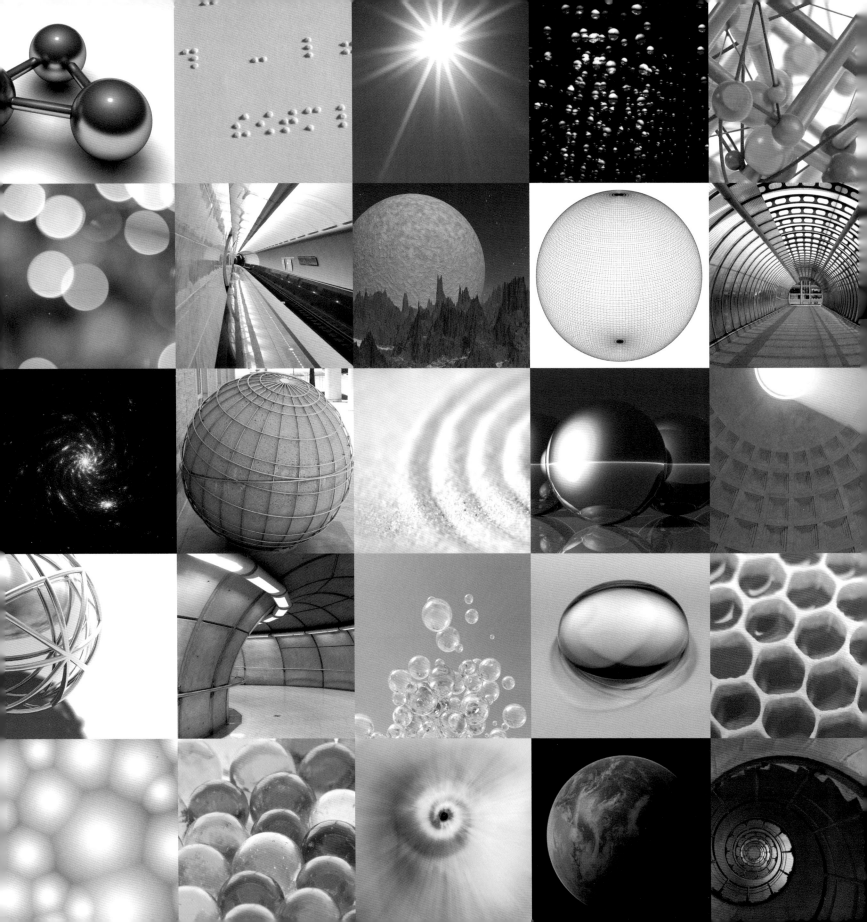

COMPETITION PHASE

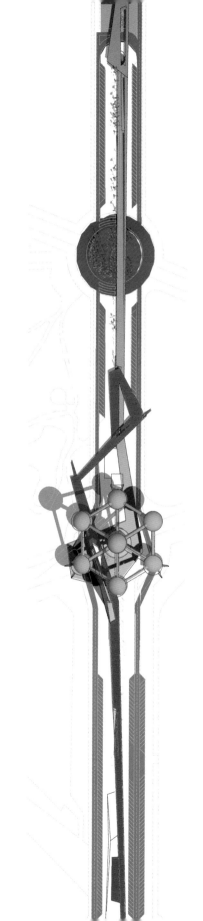

023

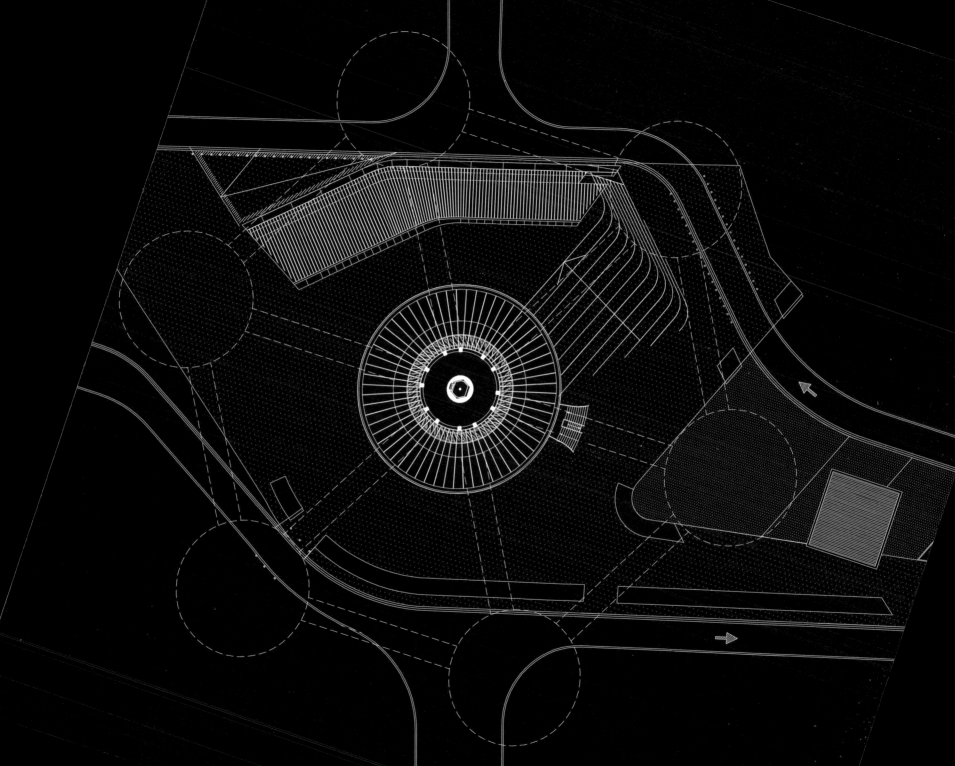

CONTINUOUSLY IN MOTION

**HISTORY** – When Christine Conix founded the office in 1979 in Wilrijk, Belgium, the architectural practice was called Architectenbureau Christine Conix. In 1989, the offices moved to Antwerp and the number of collaborators has grown ever since. Conix Architects (since 2002) is run by Christine Conix and Sylvie Bruyninckx, who became a partner in 2005. A team of 67 creative and motivated collaborators form a solid structure both at the Antwerp based head office and the office in Brussels (since 2004).

Conix Architects has grown steadily over the years, but its expansion has gained momentum the last couple of years. The size and budgets of the projects have increased over the years as well as the experience of both architects and their collaborators. Landmark projects include the modern master residence in the historic Cogels Osylei in Antwerp (1992) and the renovation and expansion of the Atomium in Brussels (2005). Developing office buildings, apartments, housing and urban concepts form the basis of the architects' activities. Designing individual houses is viewed as their building laboratory, thus helping them to stay in touch with real living and building needs which have to be continuously examined, explored and refined. Conix Architects do not restrict their client base to Belgium but also work abroad e.g. in France, the Netherlands, Luxembourg and Italy.

**PROFILE** – The projects we take on are both residential such as private homes, housing complexes, apartments as well as schools, cultural projects, commercial buildings, offices, banks, industrial projects, interior design, property development and renovations. It is a conscious decision not to specialize in a specific sector: every project offers its own challenges.
The nature, extent or budget is not a determining factor when deciding to take on a project, but rather whether it would be possible to initiate a dialog with the client who is open to contemporary and stylish architecture. The needs, wishes and expectations of the client are translated into buildings with a unique appearance drawn from contemporary concepts, displaying the highest quality of work.
These ideas reflect the uniqueness of our work, as it strives to explore the guiding principles of spaciousness, communication between indoor and outdoor spaces, refinement and perfection.
We as Conix Architects do not strive to design buildings with a unique style per definition but try first of all to meet the needs of the client. These ideas reflect the uniqueness of their work as it strives to achieve its guiding principles of spacious- ness, communication between the indoors and outdoors, refinement and perfection.

**VISION** – The type of architecture we strive to create holds a meaningful answer for a specific position in space and time, always characterized by its open spatial concept and its sharpness. The outward appearance of the design has to reflect its content. At Conix Architects we use this duality to create lucidity for the building, which is also expressed in its relation with external and interior spaces. Functionality is essential; experiencing the internal and external spaces should evoke surprise, questions and tranquility.

**ADDED VALUE** – The collective identity of our team forms the foundation of our vision and thus the added value to achieve a successful result. The architectural added value revolves around the following aspects:

### Context and surroundings are keys

Every project requires that we understand its soul, made up of its orientation, topography, and geometrics, but also the spirit of the time e.g. trends and the economic climate. The architecture has to contribute to its surroundings in the broadest or any sense and add aesthetic and cultural value to society and the individual's life.
'We must move with the times.'

### Long-term sustainability as the key

Sustainability in the long run is essential for the intangible side of architecture in physical terms such as the choice of substantial elements (e.g. location and choice of materials), but also in emotional (e.g. atmosphere, light and shadow) and intellectual aspects (e.g. debate and culture). Sustainable building shows respect for the environment and a long-term architectural vision.
'To be timeless, we strive to build for future generations.'

### Image and experience of the firm are keys

As we are attuned to human needs both relating to preconditions and user conditions for the built-up and imagined space, we develop one specific concept: namely searching, processing and exchanging information to help one see and feel architecture. That encapsulates the societal dimension of Conix Architects.
'Architecture moves people and evokes emotion.'

### Know-how combined with business acumen

Experience has taught us how to approach every project at its best, how to choose the right partners, control the economic aspect efficiently and approach the project in a multidisciplinary way. Imagination and resourcefulness are the strength that we apply to meet with quality and budgetary needs. We value the input of every intervening member. All of these efforts lead to attractive and high quality results.
'Budget inputs are subject to output evaluations in quality.'

**Our primary task at Conix Architects is building outstanding concepts, irrespective of their size or difficulty, to the best of our abilities. The result is always plural and never remote from its specific expectations, needs and objectives.**

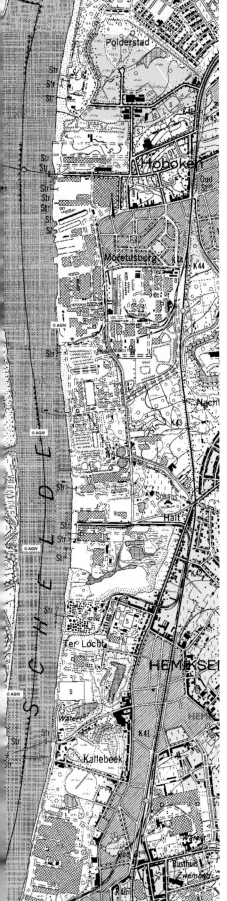

Client: Umicore nv – Date: 2005 – Area: 110 ha / 270 ac

## 002. UMICORE

MASTERPLANNING OF AN INDUSTRIAL SITE AND OFFICE BUILDING, HOBOKEN (NEAR ANTWERP)

The company plant of Umicore, south of the Antwerp agglomerate, is part of a larger industrial park. The site is a city in itself but lacks structural cohesion and coherence. Conix Architects had to structure this complex site to promote a new corporate identity. In order to integrate the plant better into its surroundings and generate an improved feeling on the whole, reconversion was considered.

Conix Architects developed a strategy which creates a new and more accessible identity for the company. The strengths and weaknesses of the terrain were determined. Based on this, Conix Architects drew up a master plan, including the problem areas and particular issues. The master plan points out the complexity and diversity of the necessary actions. Consequently, the perception and emotions of future visitors and employees are also considered. The functionality and flow of logistical activities are revised and modified, where needed.

Multiple spatial changes are made: adding a compact tower building with offices, screens, green areas, billboards, signage and route descriptions and the renovation of a number of important industrial buildings.

The new office building is the eye-catcher, encapsulating and generating the company's new corporate identity. It offers a place to stop on the main axis which runs through the entire site. By narrowing and shaping the street profile, the idea of an entry area is created, an element that was lacking. The office building is unrestrained in design in contrast to the monotonous and randomly selected surroundings. The design draws one's attention, in an emotional response, counter to the existing rational background. By positioning the building at a slight angle, the axis of the central entry road is broken.

The powerful, high-tech look and feel creates an innovative image, thus modernizing the company. Umicore is ready to face the 21st century as a dynamic and innovating company.

043

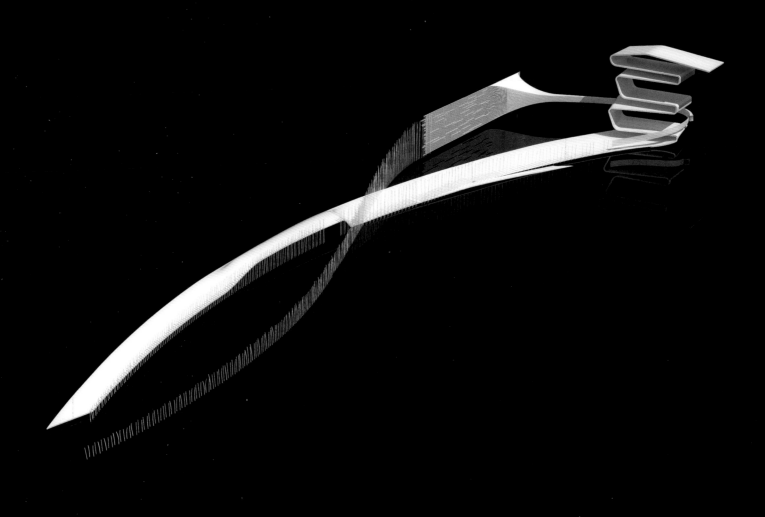

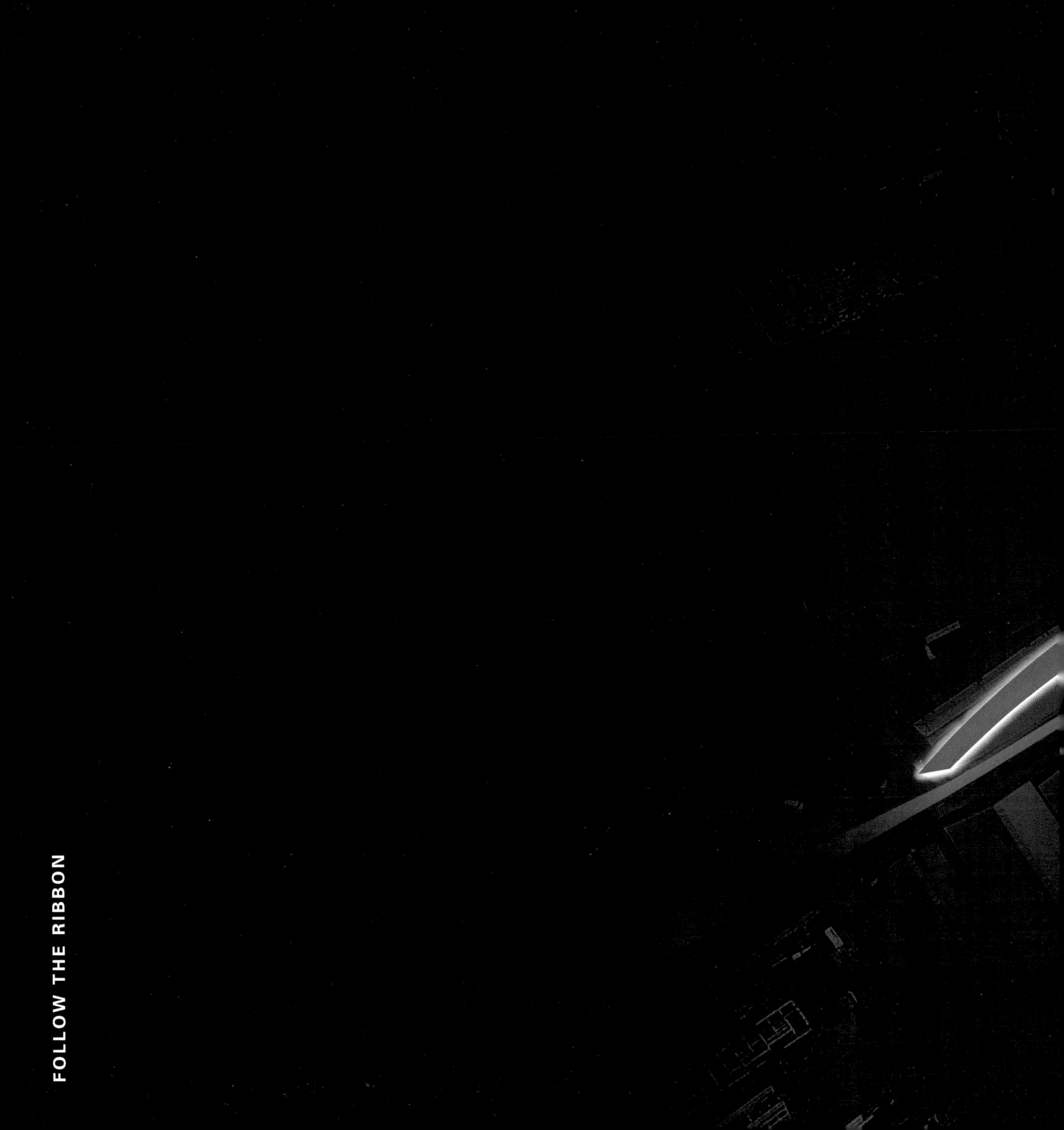

# FOLLOW THE RIBBON

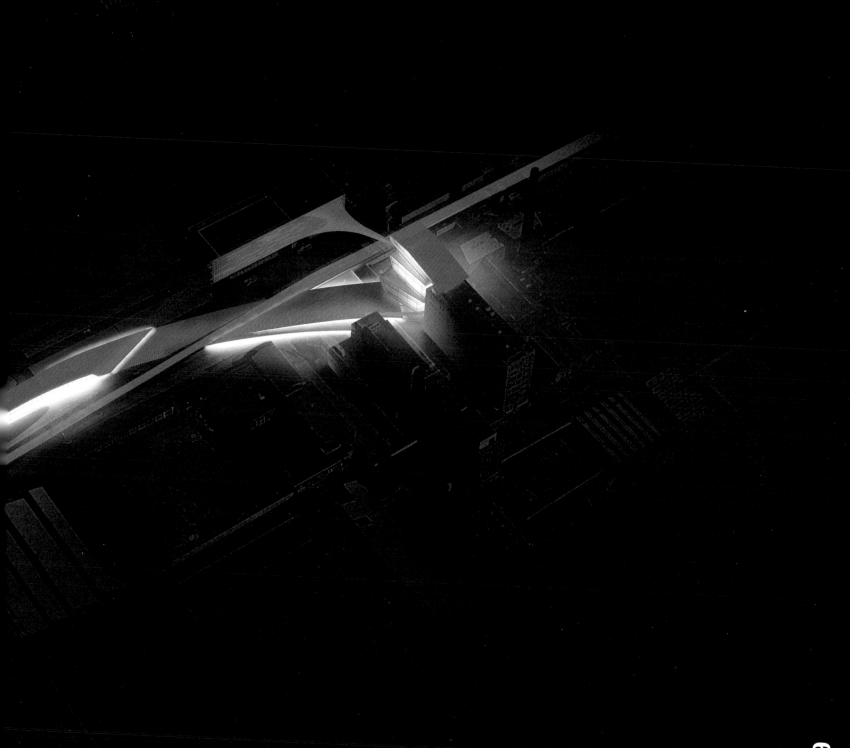

Client: Atenor nv – Date: 2005 – Area: 86.000 m² / 925,700 sq ft

This site is located along a road that approaches Brussels from the north, near the Gare du Nord (North Station) in an urban area which is in the process of being completely transformed. A canal and skyscraper set the scene, creating a mixed context of industrial and urban beauty. Conix Architects created a bold statement, where two towers rise up and serve as landmarks for the area.

The program is divided in two parts: offices and apartments on the higher level, shops, bars and restaurants on the lower level expressed by a 'void'. The aim is to combine two scales: the city (urban scale) and the neighborhood (human scale). The urban scale is represented by two towers of differing heights. The façades are designed to act as structural and aesthetic elements that duplicate the pattern of crossing lines visible on the floor plans. These lines generate continuity between vertical and horizontal parts of the building and also strengthen the links with the industrial character of the site.

The office entrance is visible from the main street; the apartments have breathtaking views of the canal. All levels have been designed to offer a flexible floor plan, which allows for different layouts and arrangements.

The human scale is represented through public spaces on the ground floor (shops) and the first floor (esplanade with pavilions) of the building, which offer a space to host festivities and cultural events. The patios of the offices allow light to penetrate and create vertical viewpoints throughout the building. The ground floor is pene-trated by several openings, which allow for numerous framed views from the street to the canal.

In combining the different scales it creates an interweaving pattern of functions that are projected in plan and elevation. By doing so, the occurrence of the built environment becomes a crossing-over event between a multitude of actions and motions taking place.

RESEARCH

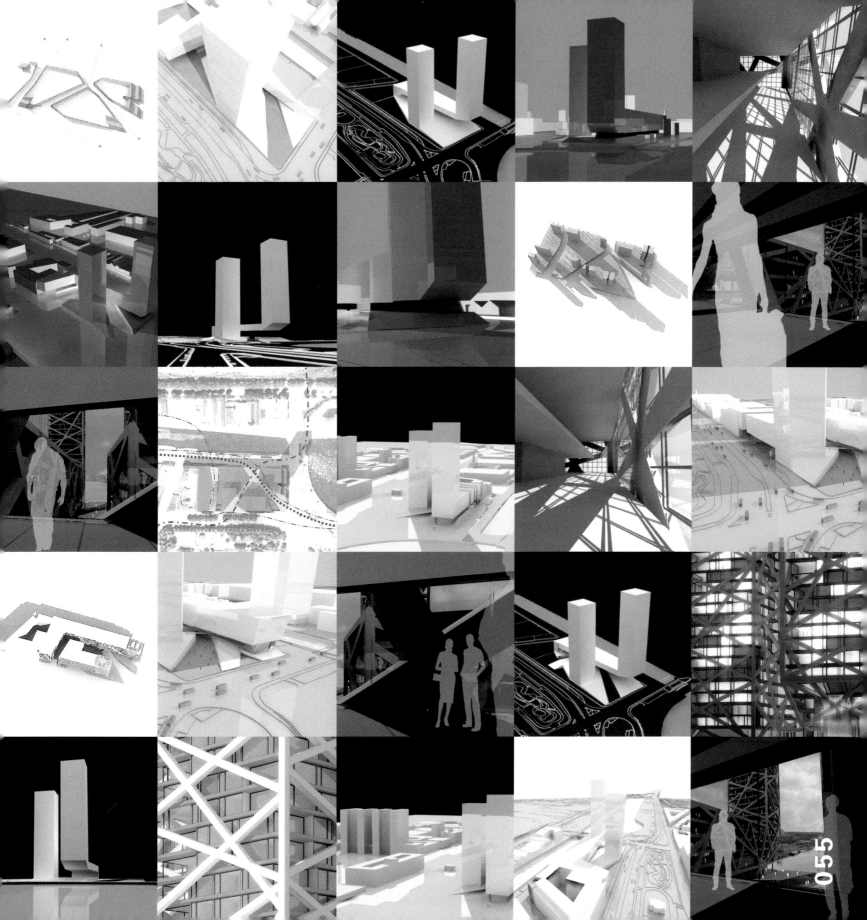

Architects have a tendency to endorse the value of their solutions and deliberately show how their buildings best meet real or assumed needs, make the most of the financial limitations and some even succeed in interpreting specific historic situations and subjective or collective desires.

After visiting numerous Conix buildings, I realized that Conix Architects use architecture as an instrument which translates the forms and organization of the environment into a series of specific values, on which the decisions are made in conjunction with the client. The technical formal and aesthetic language of Conix's architecture transmits – by means of the rational and emotional input of the team and the client – a fixed value in the daily use of the building.

Conix Architects do not build works of art, monuments or cultural prototypes but their design is unmistakably interesting, valuable and an attractive element in its surroundings. This text is evidence of my enthusiasm and a preliminary comment on their creations as I am sure that their work represents many layers of meaning yet unbeknown to me.

**CONTEXT** – *'Every project is about understanding the soul of a place but also the spirit of the time.'*

Architecture is inescapable. Everyone is confronted with or subjected to it: now and forever. The idea that an architect or a team does some research at the start of a project and then consciously conceives a strategy that leads to a design is positive and shows a conscious engagement with the environment. Conix Architects interpret the environment not only in terms of atmosphere, light and shadow but also orientation, topography, geometry, ecology and quality of life.

When conducting an environment inspection, Conix Architects analyze the site in terms of orientation or symmetry but also its residential value or aesthetic. We can thus assume that they work within the formalist model, in other words, showing 'architectural concern' for visual characteristics of a building, and giving a lot of graphical and descriptive attention to the presentation stage of the design sketches, drafts and models. As their clients are primarily from the private sector, they have to respond quickly to design, briefing and budgetary changes. This makes them the most important pawn, responsible for maintaining the quality of the building and its surroundings.

Their architecture, which grows within current trends and tastes, is not unique, original or extraordinary but rather a unique answer to a client's wishes and testimony to their strong belief in their competence. Architecture conceived by two women and the inclusion of multiple aesthetic considerations by them, are reflected in the end result. Their design partly responds to the needs of the client or real estate developer, and partly to the design methodology. A building's autonomy in terms of a program is an essential part of their architecture.

Conix Architects do not subscribe to an academic approach and do not want to be known for a unique or specific style. They treat architecture as something precious but also alluring, which means that a lot of attention is paid to visual features, play of lines, façades, volume control and form. As all of this is linked to various rules which have to be respected, the uniqueness of a place is highlighted and thus determines the value of its architecture.

**SUSTAINABILITY** – *'If time is a key, it has to be expressed physically in the choice of material elements, as well as emotionally and intellectually by reconciling architecture with construction'.*

The idea that architecture is a form of art and the architect an artist does not wash with Conix Architects. Their approach is too rational, systematic, transparent and efficient. By using simple images and communication, they emphasize the seriousness of the building process and those elements which have to support living or working in that building. Space and dimension play an important role in achieving this but also the sustainability of space, division and relationships in time. Their spaces are well thought-out and their buildings are, more often than not, able to adapt to changes.

They see modernization not as a bill of quantity but a judgment call: deciding on forms and materials in a calculated manner. Every design follows a predetermined pattern, starting with physical outlines followed by emotional input, and projected against a schedule that includes the conceptualization, construction and handing over phases.

Christine Conix and Sylvie Bruyninckx are fascinated by attractive, appealing, aesthetic architecture. One could even say that elegance drips from their fingertips when it comes to architecture: creating natural and flowing designs. This compliment is often uttered by many of their critics, fans, colleagues and clients.

Their architecture engages in a positive dialog between man and his environment. It does not dominate but stands out because of its unobtrusiveness, abundance of form and – the last couple of years – use of contrasting material such as black brickwork. Their architecture is discrete yet deliberately warm, standing out from its surroundings because of its controlled and distinguished appearance.

Their work is less known for its surprising aspect but rather for attention to detail, a characteristic Conix touch. Although they have been taking on larger projects over the years, the scale is limited. However, they impress with high quality and distinct, attractive architectural design. Their buildings are often the highlight in a street, housing or office area. Obviously, conceptualizing and realizing architecture in terms of formal representation is a common approach.

**SOCIAL DIMENSION** – *'When it comes to preconditions and user conditions for the building and the surrounding space, a specific concept is drawn up on a human scale. They seek, process and transmit information to enable one to understand and feel the design.'*

Building is part of a societal system and thus reacts to developments in that system. For this reason, the results of building are closely linked to socio-economic conditions. A built-up area presents a mix of brick and nature and, therefore, architecture and urban planning are pre-eminently public issues. Because of this, it is important that architects explain their methods and architectural values in detail.

We can say that Conix Architects are receptive, and lead by means of dialog, sometimes even a bit stubbornly, if the need arises. First of all, they deem it necessary to talk to the client. In a large team this is essential as ideas have to be concretized after conceptualizing and planning. Drafting comes to an end and dialog ensues until building starts.

Many well-known Flemish (Belgian) architects adore minimalism, so much so that it has become trendy in Belgium. However, Conix Architects have never used it for this reason but rather as a sign and natural evolution and development of their style. Minimalism is not avoided but interpreted and applied, depending on the building. Over the years, the firm has subscribed to an austere style and straightforward approach. Creating abundant and appropriate incidence of light and large, open volumes is typical of their work. Their current work reflects the hugely popular design trend for incorporating architectural sculptures and sculptural architecture.

The fact that not everyone finds a building attractive should not be an argument to denounce its design. Unattractiveness has never been a deciding factor in rejecting the architecture. If it is uninhabitable, it's a different story altogether. In this regard, Conix Architects use strict criteria such as human scale and quality of design, material and finishing.

The good thing about a Conix building is that it is attractive – which laymen may not realize spontaneously – and respects pure architectural standards. One can immediately recognize them wherever they may be. Not because they are overwhelming but rather because of their lines, volume, relations, openings, heights, choice of material and finishing. Quality is never compromised but a given within their style.

As such, they provide an answer to society's question regarding the nature of architecture. They see it as playing with forms whilst controlling them. It is a design language which one has to learn to appreciate, as you would art. The precision and purity they apply in their design is clearly reflected in the details such as brickwork, shadow gap, deep-set frames, verticality, fitted plinths, and blind doors.

To them architecture has to be approached in an honest way: they look for the right solutions in a methodical way. They don't want to shock because people have a great need to keep their surroundings familiar. Made to measure does exist in architecture, especially when dealing with inexperienced clients.

**KNOW-HOW** – *'Due to years of experience, we know how to choose the right mode of procedure, appropriate study partners, apply good budgetary control, and a multidisciplinary approach. Our strength lies in our inventiveness and imaginativeness which means that quality does not have to be more expensive.'*

It is possible to find original ideas anywhere in the world because of global economy and an internationally minded culture within an architect firm. Local differences in formulating and applying certain accents together with the unique characteristics of the local building industry contributed to Conix's own vision. Fundamental knowledge of design techniques, vast creative resources and the client's social responsibility form the parameters within which the firm practices architecture.

Every building is the result of hundreds of decisions made in quick succession which have to be continuously streamlined to keep costs under control, if the desired result is to be achieved. There is a reason for every decision the architect takes. The reason and its execution determine the quality of the architecture. Quality cannot be separated from the building and its surroundings, but is part of it and becomes visible. Making architectural quality visible requires that the architect communicates the possibilities of how the design can function within a specific context, environment and predetermined parameters.

One can find numerous reviews of films or plays but finding a review of architecture or a new building – which will last much longer and have a greater, long-term impact on society – is much rarer. This appears rather negative, as a lack of criticism comes across as a lack of norms and quality standards, which then leads to the deterioration of cultural quality and architecture.

In this sense, Conix Architects see building as a way of communicating within a given societal system. Communication implies that both the client and architects demand certain things, such as listening to each other, also within their own team. They demand clear formulations, and relations to unify and grow into an end result. That result cannot be judged based on static or valueless ideas about architecture. Experience and multidisciplinarity influence a concept but does not take precedence over a team's creativity. Already, one feels that the creativity of new partners, in conjunction with international style influences, will determine the oeuvre of Conix Architects in future.

Moniek E. Bucquoye

Moniek E. Bucquoye (BE) has 25 years of experience in the field of architecture and design, specializing in the period 1980 to the present. She has made significant contributions to the recognition of Belgian architecture and design. Her career has encompassed editing, writing, teaching, conference lectures, curating, consulting, and broadcasting. She was the inspiration, author or co-author of several books and authored numerous essays for magazines, catalogs and books.

Client: Bank J. Van Breda & Co nv – Date: 2003 - 2006 – Area: 12.500 m² / 134,550 sq ft

On this site one finds the former Goederenstation Zuid, a building that fell into disuse during the 1960s. In its heyday it was the epicenter of transport for people and goods. When the southern dockyard reached its maximum capacity, harbor activities moved to the northern docks and the station thereafter became derelict. In 1998 the station was declared a national monument for its rich maritime and industrial archeological value. When Conix Architects visited the building for the first time they realized that it possessed a rich and layered history and appointed themselves as guardians who had to clear the cobwebs of time, in an effort to re-store the building to its former glory. Along with upgrading the site and the building, Conix Architects also had to design new offices. The renovated station building and the new offices became the headquarters of Bank J. Van Breda.

This project is located in Antwerp's Nieuw Zuid (New South), an area that is currently being upgraded, near the recently completed Palace of Justice designed by architect Richard Rogers.

The position of the new office building is inspired by the master plan for Nieuw Zuid and the urge to contrast the old building with the new building. The existing building houses the reception area, counters, small auditorium and office spaces.
The new section will be used for open-space offices. The two buildings are connected by light and transparent skyways, which symbolize the transition from old to new, a constant reminder when you move between buildings.

The golden thread in this design lies in the tension between the newly added elements and the original structure. The new building, however, will always be of secondary importance to the historical goods station in terms of volume and materials. By lowering the existing rear wall, the new building and the station building interact; the unity of the entire complex and the corporate identity of the bank are reinforced in this way. The new building reflects elements of the existing station building, in terms of height and through its unmistakable horizontal subdivision of layers. Layer by layer, a contemporary design of closed-up and deep-set open levels has been created.

The closed façade is covered in dark zinc with a patina finish; this material reinforces the contemporary interpretation of the station and reminds us of its industrial character. In this way, the entire complex gracefully integrates into its restored urban environment.

SCHELDE

LEDEGANCKKAAI

DE GERLACHEKAAI

COCKERILLKAAI

SINT-MICHIELSKAAI

PLANTINKAAI

Client: Himmos nv - Date: 1999 - 2006 - Area: 13.000 m² / 139,950 sq ft

The area between Cockerillkaai and Timmerwerfstraat looked chaotic because it lacked design unity. Due to the existing relationship between a number of large buildings – namely the Zuiderpershuis, a block of apartments on the corner and a museum (Muhka) – the perspective had already been determined by and large. Conix Architects felt compelled to put an end to this mish-mash of building styles. Their final organization of the buildings lies between urban compacting and spatial perception.

The project comprises three buildings. Block A is connected to an existing corner building, thus completing the façade line in Cockerillkaai and Timmerwerfstraat. Block C runs parallel to Timmerwerfstraat. Block B is an existing warehouse which is renovated and extended. The triangular space between the three buildings is turned into a private courtyard. Where the three buildings meet, a small, private area is formed with views of the Schelde docks, the Zuider docks and the Zuiderpershuis.

The interaction of horizontal lines on the Cockerillkaai (Block A) – interrupted by vertical strips – serves as a counterbalance to the massive structure of the Muhka museum. Conix Architects used lines more or less everywhere to unite the designs of these buildings and thus create a unique and recognizable character for the entire complex.

Only in the case of Block B – to accommodate the extension to the warehouse – a closed design was used for the north-facing façade, using materials consistent with the specific historical background of the warehouse. The horizontal detailing of the façade is limited to the two end walls.

The façades of Block A and Block C on Timmerwerfstraat are interrupted in places to make incidences of light and air possible in the sharp angle between the two streets. Consequently, the façades reflect the existing building outline of the street. Because of this design choice, Timmerwerfstraat has become more airy and spacious, in contrast to the enclosed and massive façade of the social housing on the other side of the street.

Block B in Leuvenstraat repeats the horizontal theme but in a more fragmented way with openings. By placing the building further back – compared to the building line of the warehouse – one has a view from the Schelde docks of the towers of the Zuiderpershuis. By not connecting the building to the enclosure and using mostly glass for the ground floor, the Zuiderpershuis can be seen in its totality. The detailed construction of the end wall on the Waalse Kaai opens up the Leuvenstraat, allowing for a clear view of the entrance to the Muhka. Conix Architects created recreational spaces here with water features and stepping stones.

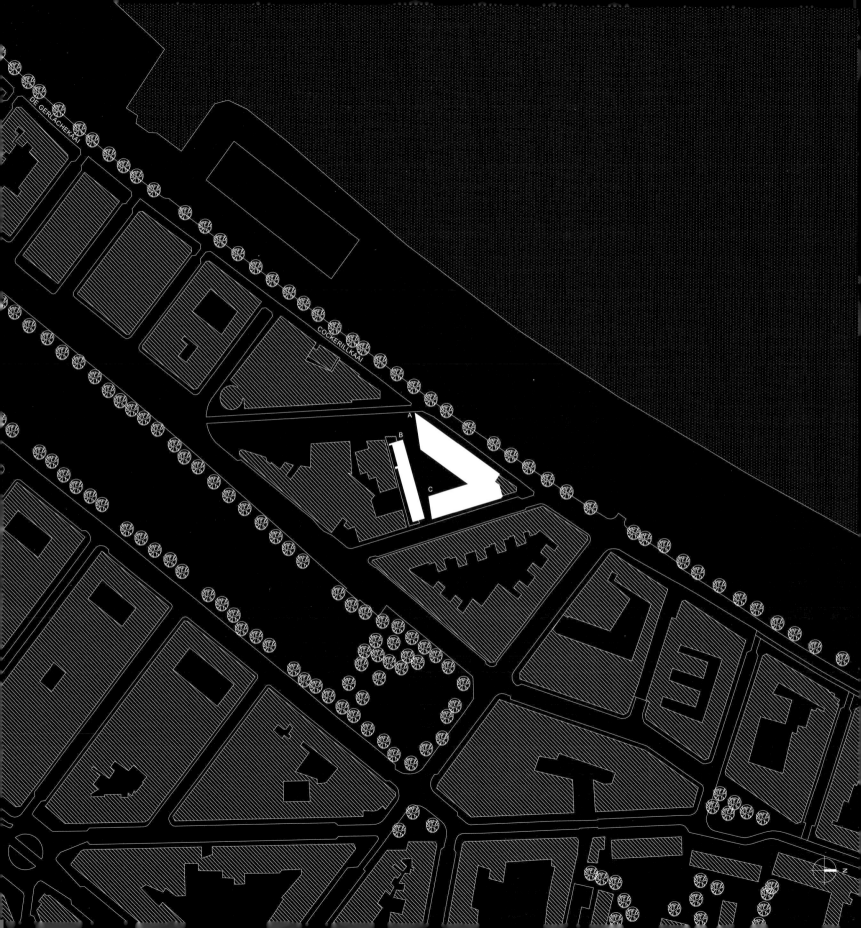

Client: Privacy Policy – Date: 2003 - 2005 – Area: 325 m² / 3,500 sq ft

This family home can be described as a functional, austere whole, tailored to the client's needs, incorporating the specific subdivision requirements. The rectangular volume has a strong presence on the side facing the street, and is illuminated with cutouts in a few places. Proportional relationships of the cantilever and window compositions were closely examined in function of light entry and spatial experience. The entry hall is dominated by glass surfaces, behind which integrated wood cupboards line the walls, thus corresponding to the unity of the façade.

In this way, the front-facing façade forms an exceptionally strong unity, encapsulating the essence of the brick architecture. Once inside, the connections between the various rooms are noteworthy. The spaces are linked by an S-shaped circulation through the layout, through which the space on the terrace becomes optimally integrated

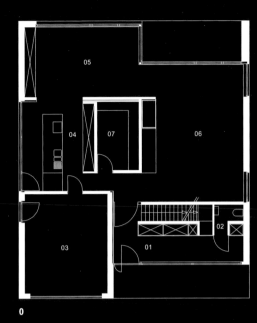

0

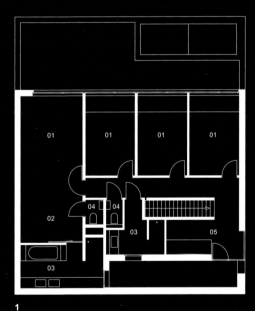

1

N

'There are no rules of architecture for a castle in the clouds.' — GILBERT K. CHESTERTON

689

In collaboration with: Archi2000 bvba, DMV bv, AST cvba, M&R nv - Client: Privacy policy - Date: 2004 - Area: 57,000 m² / 613,550 sq ft

# 007. EDUCATIONAL CENTER
## SCHOOL BUILDING, BRUSSELS

Not far from Brussels, one finds some run-down buildings, in dire need of renovation. The existing structures form a cohesive entity with an impressive character, embedded in its urban surroundings as an important landmark.

For the purposes of this competition, Conix Architects wanted to find a more suitable and manageable concept. Bearing the future users in mind, they encapsulated what people understand by the concept of 'identity' or more specifically, European identity. The conclusion was that the strength of Europe's identity lies in its variety. Socio-cultural differences generate fascinating tensions between people and where they live. Conix Architects focused on specific parameters such as language and cultural diversity. Conscious of romanticizing this concept of diversity, they looked into different ways of designing spaces and buildings which would generate the ability to accommodate and support cultural variety.

The point of departure at Conix Architects has always been modernistic, based on functionality and rationality. In the first place, every design starts off as a neutral base to which the basic outlines of all requirements are added. In the second place, emotion is taken into account, namely the user's perception of the design. The proposal focused on this aspect and so generated an image which coincided with that of the school. Then this feeling was applied to the spatial organization, regarding the scale of the site and the individual buildings. Variety seemed possible by creating a rational framework, mentally and physically.

This is translated into sober buildings, contradicting the existing architecture, resulting in a serene composition. A number of playful and dynamic elements were also added. These elements set the whole in motion, thus generating the idea of subtle diversity.

The frame of the central volume clears the way to the city, creating a direct link with the skyline (macro scale) but also serves as a landmark and center within the site (micro scale). The massive scale of this center (e.g. frame, central stairs and open square) which a child is confronted with as he enters, is replaced by a more intimate scale (e.g. patios and smaller stairs) as he approaches the classroom. The center connects the three clusters (kindergarten, primary and high school), which, in turn, were built around paths or patios. In this way, the school unifies different elements, each of which keep their own identity. These elements are not clearly demarcated but flow into one another.

The variety of buildings generate numerous spatial sensations and moods, for instance, the staircase in the closed cylinder leads to the dining hall in the open frame. The variety of spatial perceptions, colors, materials, textures and scales (interior and exterior) allows the architecture to fulfill its pedagogical role. The transparent and airy nature of the spaces is very important as nothing is concealed. Within the buildings, the scale and size of children per age group are taken into account. For instance, in the kindergarten section, some windows are positioned at the height of the average child of this age. The choice of color is also determined by age groups: primary colors are used in the kindergarten section and subdued colors for the high school.

UNITED, NOT BY ONE LANGUAGE BUT BY THE DIVERSITY OF ALL PRESENT LANGUAGES AND CULTURES.

Client: Sibelga cvba – Date: 2005 - 2006 – Area: 3.600 m² / 38,750 sq ft

The head office of Sibelga, close to Brussels Gare du Nord (North Station), is housed in a building with a lot of character that was built in a typical 1970s style. The concrete façade and rigid canopy at the entrance remind Conix Architects of the heyday of constructivism. Although the building had retained its distinctive character, some parts needed to be restored and reorganized. Given the background of the building, Conix Architects had to find solutions to meet the needs of the current owners. The most significant changes included redecorating the work and meeting rooms and redesigning the reception spaces. By doing this, the flexibility of spaces was increased and the representativity of the company emphasized.

The requirements are interpreted in a clear and dynamic way. The third floor is designed to serve as the 'template'. Closed work spaces are situated next to the outer walls, offering maximum flexibility; meeting spaces are placed in the middle zones as free-standing structures, with a rotation of axes.

This creates a dynamic in the circulation spaces and additional secondary connections between both sides of the building. The meeting room gets daylight as the inner walls are transparent.

On the second floor, the system's flexibility is clearly demonstrated. A central area is created in the landscape office by placing cabinets strategically to separate functional zones. In the directors' office area, the interior design contributes to the flexibility. The reception is situated near the façade, the longitudinal façade. Next to the reception, one finds the modular room which can be opened up.
The meeting rooms can be completely opened up to lead into the modular room, to become a large differentiated space that can be used for parties, exhibitions, seminars, presentations, etc. The layout of the offices is identical to those on the third floor, whereby daylight can penetrate the middle zone.

Every floor has its own identifying color. Different shades of that color are applied to accentuate the reception and informal areas, the small kitchen, and curtains. The light shining from the building is colored, thus turning the building into a landmark in the street.

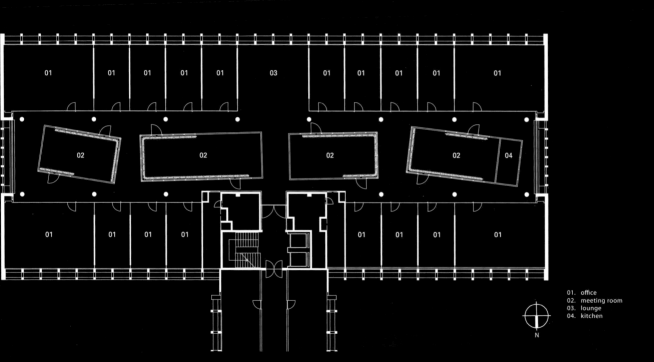

01. office
02. meeting room
03. lounge
04. kitchen

N

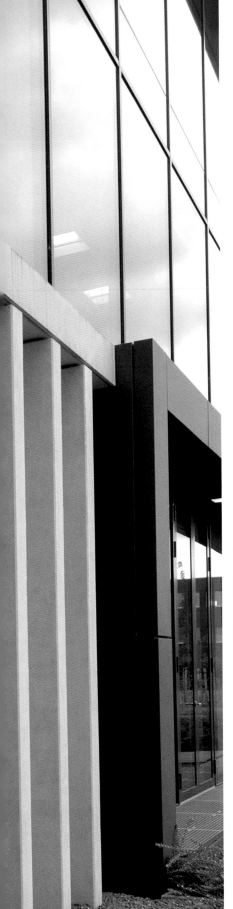

Client: OM Partners nv - Date: 2002 - 2005 - Area: 4.000 m² / 43,050 sq ft

## 009. OM PARTNERS

OFFICE BUILDING, WOMMELGEM (NEAR ANTWERP)

OM Partners is a software and consulting company. Situated in an industrial zone, an office building was designed for the specific needs of this client.

A strict division between the accessible zones for the public and the non-accessible zones led up to the conception of the plan. An L-shaped volume is created and houses besides the office function, a training zone, a research zone and spaces for supply and stock.

Particular atmospheres for the functions of this building are created. A dialog between the functions on the one hand and the façades linked to them on the other hand creates a fascinating architecture, both logical and variable at the same time. The materials used for the building are restrained: light-colored profiled concrete and glass for all façades, alternating with dark plate material for protruding parts in the façade and back wall. The interior design is both contemporary and sober: white walls, small accents with green and red planes and soft touches with wood for flooring and furniture.

When approaching the building, one can discover a frame construction on the upper floors covered in dark plate material, with the directors' offices situated behind it. On the floor below, the entrance to the building is situated. This concept is repeated on the back façade, thus creating an invitation to go outside and enjoy the well-planned garden area. Near the training center, a visually private area was created by means of rhythmically placed vertical panels made of light-colored profiled concrete.

The architecture of this project is clear, offering this company a corporate identity of being modern and up-to-date, but also stable and durable at the same time.

Client: Van Den Berg nv – Date: 2001 - 2004 – Area: 3.150 m² / 33.900 sq ft

# 010. VAN DEN BERG

## EXTENSION OF AN OFFICE BUILDING, SCHELLE (NEAR ANTWERP)

This project details the design of an office building with a cafeteria, meeting rooms and archive cellar. The building has a communal entrance that leads to the new section as well as the adjacent existing office building. The layout is done in a clear design. The structure is built on the same line as the existing building but has four storeys instead of two, resulting in the new structure dominating the space. The internal functions are conveyed externally in design and choice of materials.

The communal functions such as the central hall, cafeteria and meeting rooms are on the ground and upper floors but only in the central strip in an L-shape. This shape consists of alternating transparent and opaque glass panels and is set back two meter deeper than the façade line, creating a sharp contrast to the offices on the upper floors that form a complete glass structure.

The two parts are separated by a 20-inch strip of grey concrete which forms the backbone of the building.

The transition from the building to the surroundings is sudden, showing no sign of ambiguity. By elevating the building a bit, a rigid border is created between the green grass and the rigid cement line. This can be clearly seen at the entrance and at the back. A concrete wall encloses a large terrace and obscures the view of the parking area.

Client: Privacy policy – Date: 2002 - 2004 – Area: 750 m² / 8,050 sq ft

This newly built house for a large family is located in the vicinity of Brussels. The most important characteristics of the site are the presence of a slope on the side facing the street, the southern orientation of the front façade and the presence of a magnificent oak tree. These were integrated into the design. The building volume was opened up to create a patio. This provides the whole rear of the house (main hallway, study, children's play corner and living room) with extra daylight. Additionally visual relationships were sought with the oak tree.

The volume of the house is partly moved into the slope and partly raised, creating an exciting relationship between the existing terrain and the new house. The front-facing façade is given a massive and closed design. The windows were formed through fine vertical cut-aways, with pivoting shutters to shut out the sun. The spaces on the floors – specifically the parents' bedroom and bathroom – are also afforded privacy by shutters, which can be opened or shut completely. In contrast to the closed front-facing façade, the rear façade opens up completely. This way the garden, designed by landscaping architect Erik Dhont, is integrated into the experience of the living spaces. Because of this the opened up kitchen and spacious living room are bathed in light.

Classic and natural-looking colors and materials are chosen to materialize this project. Wood, brown brick, a cream-colored marble for the flooring finish and pale oak wooden floors supply a homogenous and warm character.

Client: Beroepskrediet nv – Date: 2005 – Area: 10.000 m² / 107,650 sq ft

012. W16

RENOVATION AND EXTENSION OF AN OFFICE BUILDING, BRUSSELS

This building, designed by Hugo van Kuyck and built in 1958 for the SNCI, is situated in the commercial area boulevard de Waterloo, known for its luxury shops. It is a Y-junction of the 'small ring road', running through old parts of the city, a proper 'river of cars', surrounded by commercial enterprises and hotels in a multicultural area.

The concept for this project is based on the presence of a number of striking architectural elements. This building is reminiscent of the glorious 1960s. The combination of contemporary architecture with the existing style has breathed new life into this building. This project entails renovating the building completely as well as the Bâtiment de l'Horloge at the rear. These two structures were also linked while the enclosed inner area got an atrium.

A new façade is envisaged for the building, a commercial section on the ground floor and offices on the upper floors. While designing the façade, Conix Architects wanted it to integrate into the existing context. It became more appealing with a contemporary, new look. By using twisted glass plates a refined vertical level is created that makes the building less imposing. In this way, the building forms a fragmented resting point, dominated by a continuous flow of urban movement on the side.

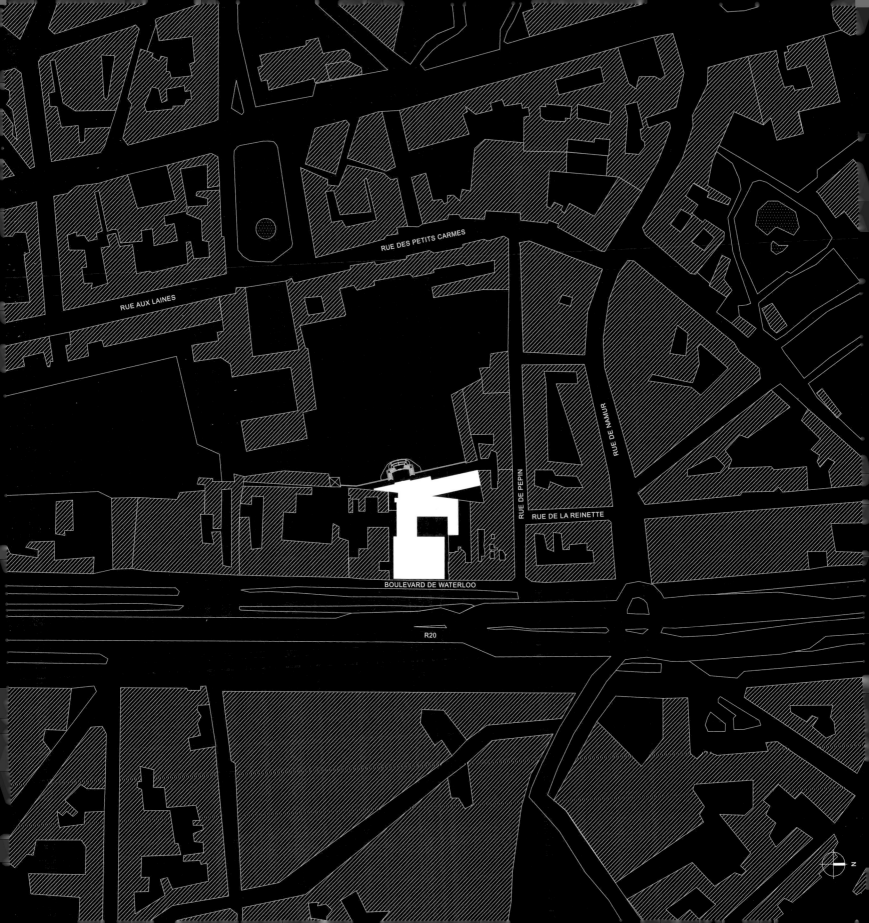

RUE DES PETITS CARMES

RUE AUX LAINES

RUE DE PEPIN

RUE DE NAMUR

RUE DE LA REINETTE

BOULEVARD DE WATERLOO

R20

N

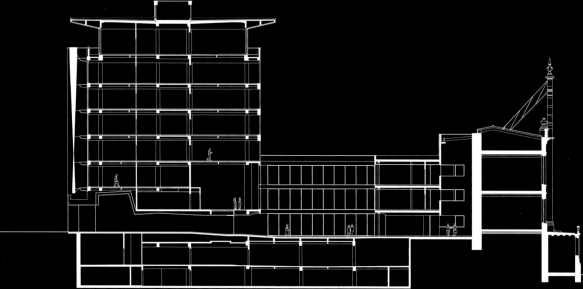

Client: Burco nv, Thomas & Piron nv – Date: 2005 – Area: 1.880 m² / 20,250 sq ft

This project site, situated in a suburb on the outskirts of Brussels, is known for its residential character but also its significant differences in height (about 13.12 feet in places). This high density area needed a spatially well-founded intervention.

Conix Architects conceptualized a building that blends into the surrounding structures in a harmonious way. By using the shape of the site and providing gardens and terraces, an airy structure surrounding a green inner courtyard is created.

This project comprises of 15 apartments and eight houses, spread over the ground floor and three upper floors. The apartments will be built in a stepped slope formation thereby keeping the height lower than that of surrounding buildings; inner areas do not get much cast shadow either. Apartments are positioned in such a way that it would not be possible to look into a neighboring apartment. The buildings are linked by means of roof terraces which can be accessed via the apartments.

The façades are covered in warm materials such as wood and light-colored plastering. The alternate open-closed character is further enhanced by these color and texture choices.

DURABILITY

'Architecture is not an inspirational business,
it's a rational procedure to do sensible and hopefully
beautiful things. That's all.' - HARRY SEIDLER

This brand-new office building for a maritime holding company is a prime example of architectural professionalism. The project is situated in one of the main and busiest roads connecting the outer ring road of the city with the center of Antwerp. The building was conceived in a no-nonsense and logical way, offering the client a flexible and sustainable building.

Large glass surfaces are framed by dark stone, creating a strong character for the building. This large frame accentuates the main function behind it, namely flexible and open office spaces. The glass surfaces which are enveloping this frame are decorated with a vibrant serigraphy print on the glass. Behind the façade on the top floor Conix Architects created a terrace linked to the cafeteria. The building blends unobtrusively into its surroundings due to the simple volumetrics used under-lined by the soberness of the materials, bringing about a harmonious transition in the varying building outlines of the neighboring buildings.

In contrast to the busy road in front of the building, a nice and quiet garden offers an open view for the offices orientated to the back wall. The fire escape is housed in a freestanding vertical volume with perforated, steel cladding. This volume balances the back façade, adding a vertical and slender accent on to the otherwise horizontal character of this plane.

The interior design is corporate and efficient. The offices are light and open. Shades of grey and blue exude tranquility and calmness throughout the building.

Client: Leman Invest nv - Date: 2000 - 2004 - Area: 5,400 m² / 58,150 sq ft

**015. FRERE ORBAN**
COMPETITION - OFFICE BUILDING, BRUSSELS

Throughout the history of Brussels, the Quartier Léopold has always been an ambitious and atmospheric quarter where urban, economic and political activities come together. Nowadays it is the heart of European Union institutions.

The concept is based on some basic principles. Firstly, an entire group of buildings has been demolished, which has enabled Conix Architects to choose the height of the office floors. In addition, they have re-engineered the relationship between private and public spaces at street level. The boundary between the street and the interior is blurred. By using free forms on the street level, a transition is created, which is dominated by the continuous flow of people.

These design elements throw a new light on both sides of the transition zone, like an intelligent organism reacting to its surroundings. With this in mind, Conix Architects looked for ways to create a pleasant interior climate; they applied a double-glazed curtain wall system and a concrete mass to generate heat, to satisfy this requirement

The final product looks to the future but takes the context and the historical aspects into account. The building anticipates future needs and finds its inspiration in a society marked by variety, communication and a longing for balance

Client: Fortis Real Estate nv – Date: 2006 – Area: 25.000 m² / 269,100 sq ft

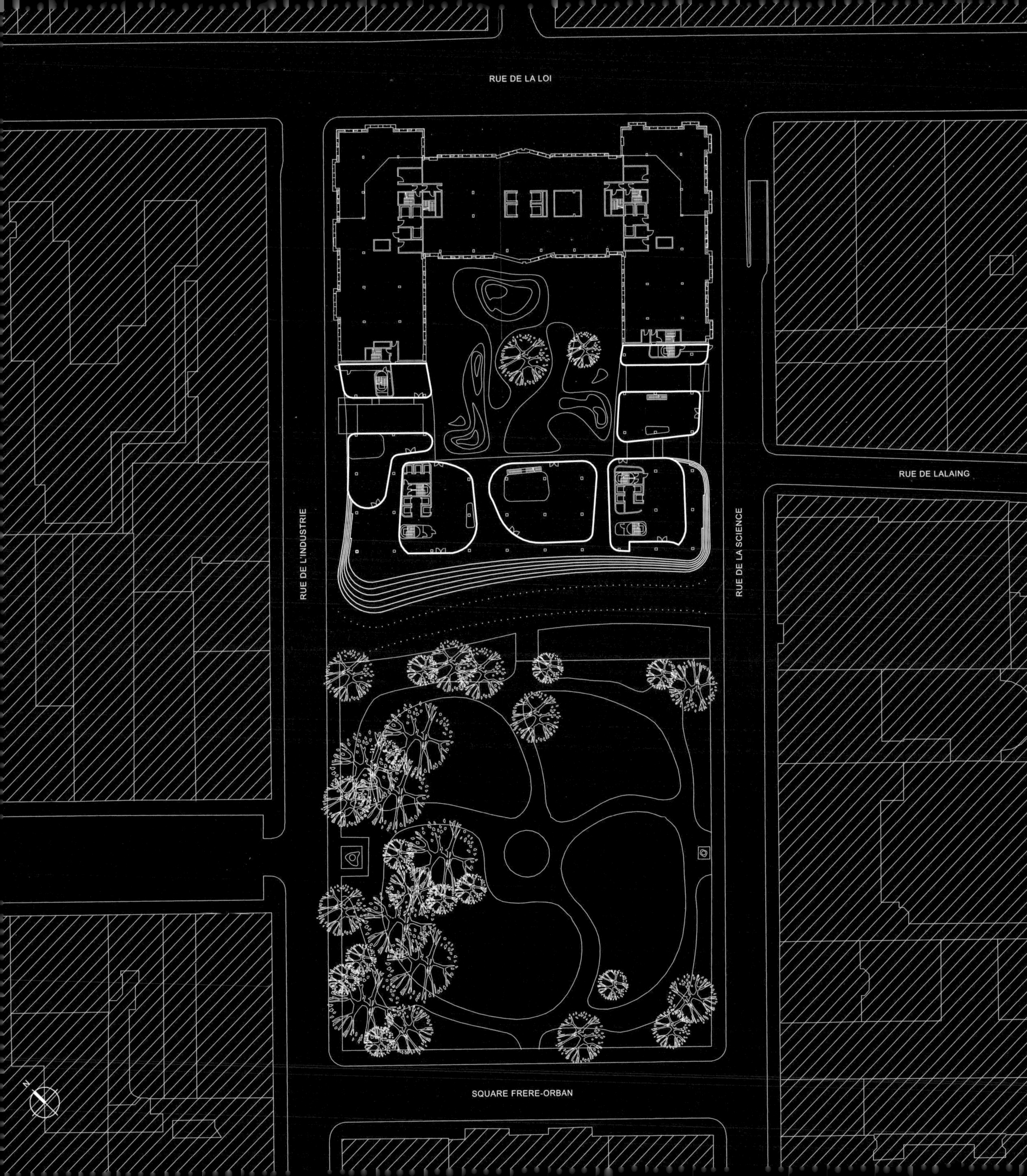

RUE DE LA LOI

RUE DE L'INDUSTRIE

RUE DE LALAING

RUE DE LA SCIENCE

SQUARE FRERE-ORBAN

143

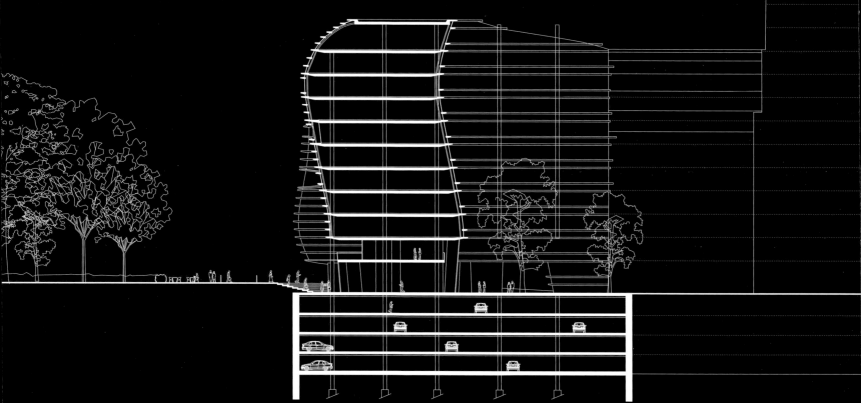

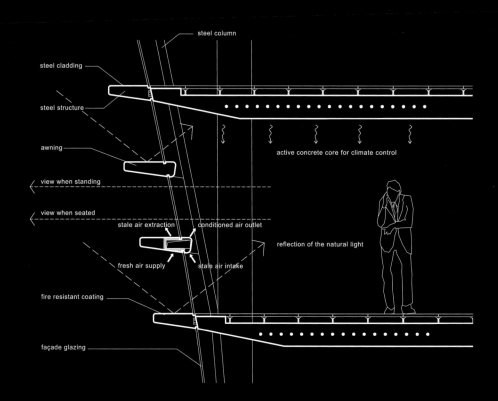

steel column

steel cladding

steel structure

awning

view when standing

view when seated

active concrete core for climate control

stale air extraction     conditioned air outlet

reflection of the natural light

fresh air supply     stale air intake

fire resistant coating

façade glazing

INSPIRED BY NATURE

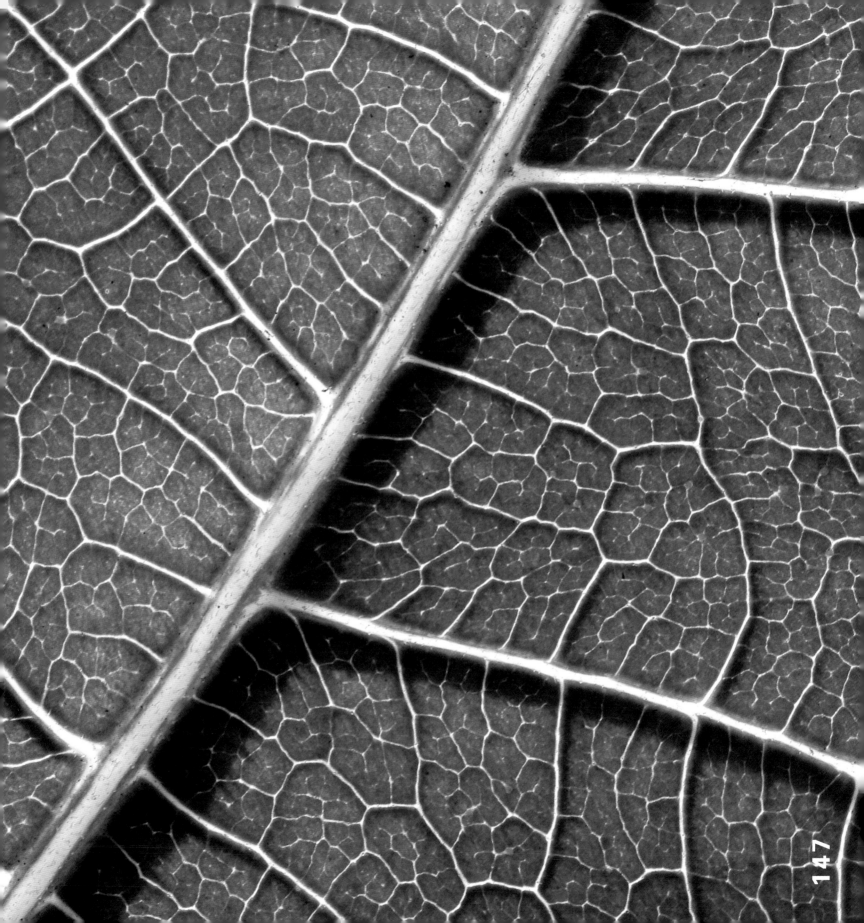

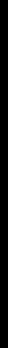

Client: Privacy policy – Date: 2005 – Area: 43.700 m² / 470.400 sq ft

This site is in an area that is currently undergoing a complete transformation. The master plan sets out to change a suburb into a residential-business area by condensing and completing a series of sites.

The master plan entails a high-rise apartment block and an adjacent smaller office block. Inspired by the modernistic viewpoint of the city of Antwerp, the building should function structurally to determine a specific, well-defined streetscape. This results in an obligatory and rigorous observance of the building line, which gives the envisaged construction a strong iconic character. It marks the starting point of an axis.

Another design criterion is met by adding a pedestrian overpass that links the building with Antwerp north. This overpass, included in the master plan, leads to an enclosed courtyard, whose atmosphere will be created by the flow of people and their work-life relationships in a city. This interaction applies to the entire site and serves as the point of departure for designing the apartments, offices and public spaces.

Conix Architects had a no-nonsense approach to designing the apartments. So, the building is styled like a sculpture that diminishes as it increases in height. In this way, the design vacillates between static stability and dynamic vanity. The designs of the adjacent inner areas and façades evolved from their relationship with the nearby water which served as inspiration. There are seven apartments on every floor; each with a different design to cater for different types of tenants. The ground floor houses an exhibition room and commercial space, in addition to apartments, as well as a visitor's pavilion. Conix Architects are turning this site into an attractive meeting place that offers a multitude of activities and atmospheres.

Client: PSA HNN nv – Date: 2003 - 2005 – Area: 5,600 m² / 60,300 sq ft

# 017. HESSE NOORD NATIE
## OFFICE BUILDING, ANTWERP

PSA HNN was formed in 2002 through the merger of two established terminal operating companies. After the merger, PSA HNN became part of the PSA group, a leading global port operator with home base in Singapore. The maritime activities of this company are both linked historical and local to this site, thus creating an extra valuable layer to this project.

When Conix Architects first visited the site, the project zone 'Het Eilandje' (the islet) had not been fully designed. It was only the beginning of the rejuvenation of the area surrounding Willemdok (Willem docks). The renovation of the Koninklijk Depot (by architect Koolhoff) signalled the start of a new era in urban development in the Antwerp North area.

This site played an important role in completing the enclosure of the entire area. The position of this building is necessary for supporting the urban look and feel of the Willemdok and the surrounding area. Hence, the specific location of this building demanded a rigid approach, in order to 'restore' and rejuvenate the neighboring environment. By erecting this office building here, Conix Architects restored the boundaries of the Willemdok and the adjacent street.

The design for this functional and flexible office building is combined with specific architectural details both in plan and in elevation. Conix Architects have implemented a fragmented scale division for the design of the façade to formulate a solution for existing and future occupants and the public alike. Light-colored stone is used for the walls, combined with a darker, rough-hewn stone. The horizontal segments correspond to those of adjacent buildings and are needed to create the requested flexible office spaces. The closed character of the façade is interrupted by a void at the entrance. This entrance area is a big double height space and opens the building up to its surroundings, thus offering this project a clear dialogue with its context.

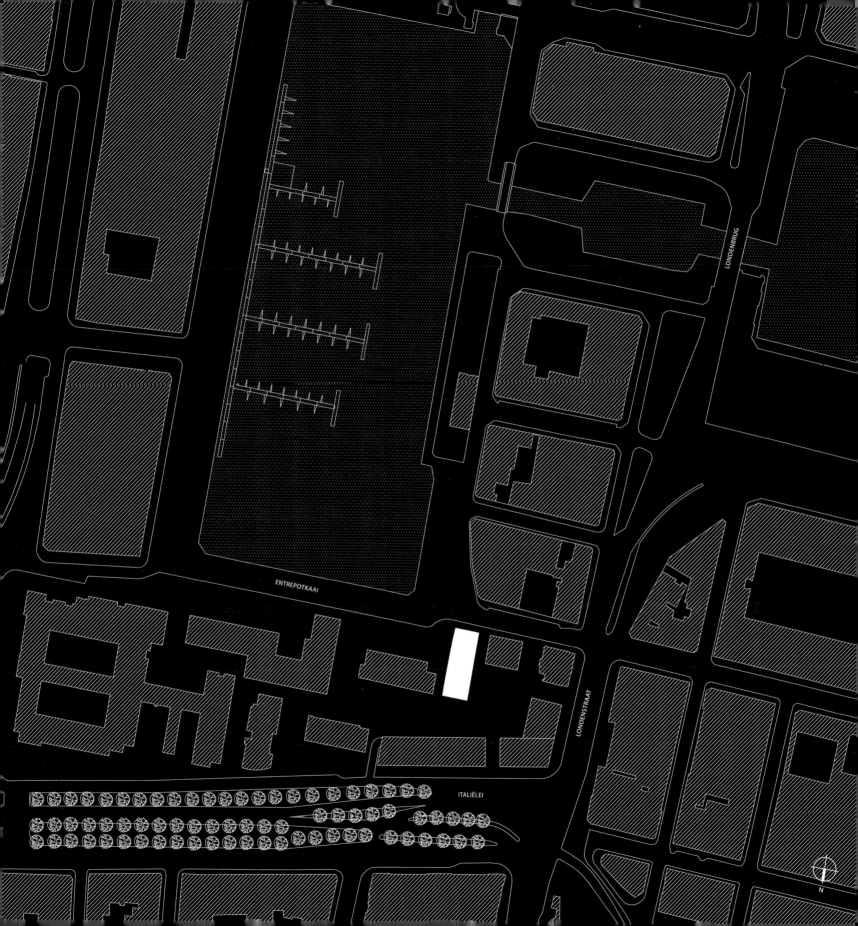

157

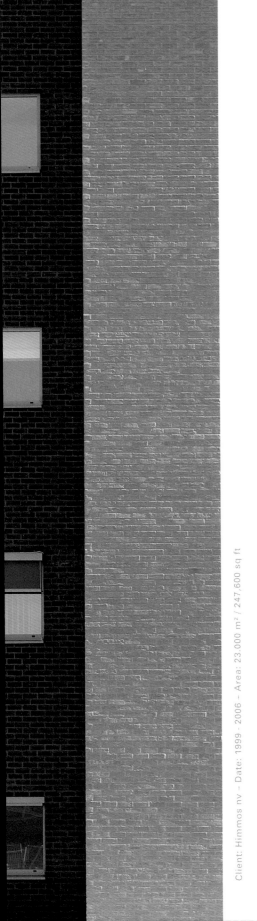

On the edge of downtown Lokeren, located on the shores of the river Durme, lies the site of a former flax mill. This district has recently been cleared and prepared as residential area.

On the opposite side of the site is a street of laborers' houses from the start of the previous century, serving as reminder of Lokeren's fascinating industrial history.

The site had enormous potential due to its perfect location and orientation. Conix Architects had the opportunity to build 121 apartments here, spread over seven buildings. They departed from a conceptual approach of optimal integration of the buildings, using a rigid architectural vocabulary. In view of the grand scale, they opted for free-standing apartment buildings. By dividing these into buildings A through G, a harmonious, contemporary whole is created, breathing new life into this area next to the Durme.

Buildings A and B, located on the shoreline of the Durme, have lead to better integration of the project into the area by building B being placed at an angle in relation to building A. These buildings consist of four storeys and a recessed top storey. This top layer of construction on buildings A and B is pushed back to keep the scale size of the buildings in check. This creates a powerful line, formed by the continuous beam. Building C forms a connection link with the existing buildings in the Koophandelstraat. Buildings D, E, F and G in Nijverheidstraat are urban villas, consisting of three levels and a top storey.

Client: Himmos nv – Date: 1999 - 2006 - Area: 23.000 m² / 247,600 sq ft

NIJVERHEIDSTRAAT

Client: Seamco nv – Date: 2004 – Area: 500 m² / 5,400 sq ft

## 019. SEAMCO
### OFFICE BUILDING, RANST-OELEGEM (NEAR ANTWERP)

Seamco manufactures machines that are used to produce reusable plastic bottles. The concept for this office building had to reflect their core business. Conix Architects' mission was to establish the logical functionality within the building and therefore light, high-tech materials were used to emphasize this aspect. The top floors are massive constructions, supported by a few concrete buttresses. In contrast, the ground floor is spacious and open.

It appears as if transparent plastic tubes support the top structure, thereby creating the impression of a floating floor.

The interior design is sober, a logical combination focusing on functionality and spatial abstraction. Bearing the exterior in mind, contrasting elements are used. Massive black elements rest on flimsy white elements, suggesting that the black elements are floating. This effect is enhanced by the white polyurethane floor. A few colorful accents in the loose furniture break the pure black-white contrast, resulting in a playful yet cohesive interior.

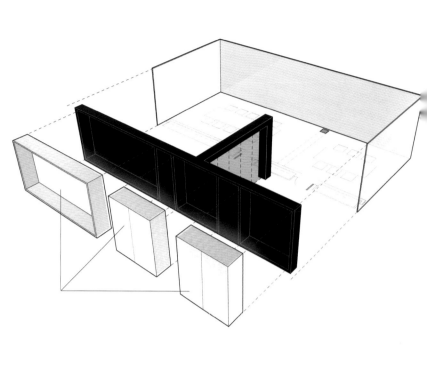

SOCIETY

'We live in a world where great incompatibles coexist:
the human scale and the superhuman scale, stability and mobility,
permanence and change, identity and anonymity,
comprehensibility and universality.' – KENZO TANGE

177

The concept for this freestanding house was derived from the characteristics of the site. The rolling landscape and forest vegetation provided the inspiration for the design. The house is immersed in its natural surroundings and relates to nature in form and function in both plan and section.

Although the structure is partially imbedded, the landscape has been respected as much as possible. The living spaces are located on an extended plinth on the first floor. This space, flooded by daylight, offers panoramic views of the green surroundings. The solid plinth on the street level houses all the services. The subdued bedrooms are located on the top floor. An integrated terrace offers yet another view of the hilly landscape.

Throughout the house, three types of material are used: slate (used for levels with supporting functions), dark brick (bedrooms) and glass (living areas). Every level is characterised by a specific type of material. The glass volume encapsulates the living areas, thus giving the inhabitants panoramic views of their surroundings.

Sustainable and ecological materials such as fibre reinforced gypsum lining board – made from gypsum and recycled paper fibres – are used for the interior finishing. In addition, solar panels and a ventilation system with a heat exchanger were installed.

Client: Privacy policy – Date: 2004 – Area: 605 m² / 6,500 sq ft

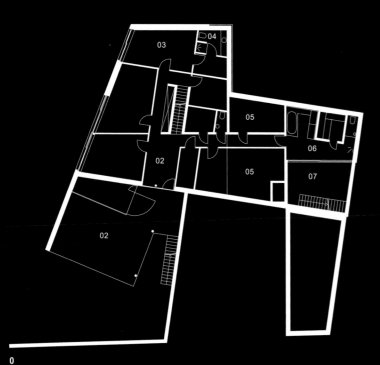

N

01. carport
02. entrance
03. guest room
04. bathroom
05. storage
06. sauna
07. patio

0

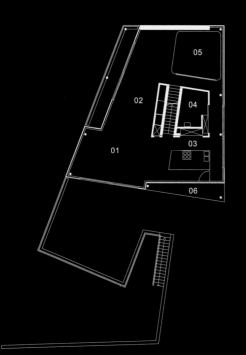

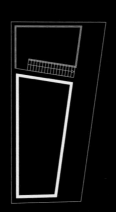

01. dining room
02. living room
03. kitchen
04. storage
05. projector room
06. terrace

1

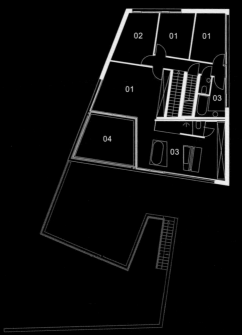

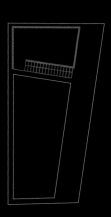

01. bedroom
02. study
03. bathroom
04. terrace

2

Client: Investimmo nv – Date: 2004 – Area: 1.600 m² / 17,200 sq ft

## 021. MERCELIS
### RESIDENTIAL DEVELOPMENT AND RENOVATION, BRUSSELS

This project entails renovating houses facing a street, building two blocks of apartments (behind the houses) and integrating a library into offices.

The volume of this development softens and improves the appearance of these buildings. In combination with the architectural intervention, the development is integrated in a transparent and airy manner behind the front houses. Conix Architects envisage two buildings, each with its own entrance and front garden. The entry axis is supported by the positioning of the buildings and the library entrance. The courtyard area becomes a hub of activities which interact with each other in different ways. The rational design of the buildings strengthens the feeling of tranquility, necessary to ensure the quality of life in an urban area.

RUE KEYENVELD

RUE SOUVERAINE

RUE MERCELIS

187

Client: Annicimmo bvba - Date: 2005 - Area: 2300 m² / 24,750 sq ft

This 19th century warehouse is one of Antwerp's classified (historical) buildings. In order to convert this industrial building into offices and luxury apartments, Conix Architects have restored it to its former glory, have upgraded and modified it to meet modern standards and needs.

Behind the building runs an inner street, flanked by buildings on both sides. This warehouse is made up of many wings that are all dilapidated. The surrounding buildings are mostly former warehouses and houses that have been turned into lofts. The existing structure and façades are slightly modified, respecting the initial design of the building.

The inner street is treated as a semi-public space that can be used by office workers and tenants. In order to stay true to its character and allow optimal light penetration, the street is kept completely open.

A particular new element in this design is the vertical ventilation duct behind the main building, positioned between two buildings as a deliberate added structure. The original footbridge between two parallel wings will be reintroduced in the new design. The ground floor serves as office space; the other floors as apartments. In this way, an old industrial building is upgraded by giving it a new function.

Conix Architects create unity by using the same materials and colors throughout. The entrance gates, window frames, parapets, glass entrance doors and lattices are all made of steel with the same anthracite color, creating an industrial look. The idea of continuity can also be seen in the interior. The industrial character of the building is reinforced by the use of open spaces, brick, steel and glass.

The tailor-made furniture, floors and ceilings create a warmer and acoustically improved living and working space. By using plasterboard and room defining furniture, instead of bricks, the space can be used in a more flexible way.

Client: Cogerimo nv, B&C – Date: 2005 – Area: 7.000 m² / 57,350 sq ft

023. BELLIARD

COMPETITION - OFFICE BUILDING, BRUSSELS

The objective of this project was to renovate an existing office block on Belliard street, one of the busiest approach roads into Brussels.

Due to several large-scale building projects and a high volume of traffic, most of the physical and optical resting spaces in the area had been consumed. Ironically, this road had once been pedestrian-friendly and linked the Palais Royale (Royal Palace) with the Cinquantenaire Park.

A further problem was that it would not be possible to break through this imaginary double wall in the middle of the city. The border separating the façade and the street was too definite and one-dimensional. A solution had to be found to facilitate the large number of pedestrians passing through each day.

By taking the scale of the building into account, it seemed obvious that such an intervention could enliven the stagnant area, where the building would become a gateway for bustling crowds. Conix Architects also looked for ways to get the street to interact with the design, so that the building could become part of the surrounding activities. To get the scale of the building correct, Conix Architects suggested fragmenting the scale of the passers-by. In a similar way, they wanted to generate an image of variety and multiculturalism, reflecting the atmosphere in the EU quarter.

At the start of the design process, Conix Architects conducted an extensive evaluation of the site's possibilities. The first study took on a radical view of changing the uninviting character of Belliard street, which led to an object with a closed façade but an unmistakable look. Finally, Conix Architects realized it would be very difficult to combine particular aspects such as flexibility, maintenance, spaciousness and functionality with this deconstructivist approach.

The final design focuses on the spatial perception, powerful exterior, internal functionality, accessibility and increase in volume. The fragmentation of the façade on different scales creates a varied composition, in stark contrast with its monotonous surroundings.

Client: Van Belle Family – Date: 2006 – Area: 8.400 m² / 90.400 sq ft

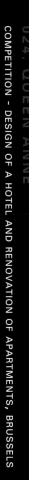

The requirement for this competititon was to build a new three-star hotel with 80 rooms. The family Van Belle-Hermans wanted a new brand hotel in the center of Brussels near their existing hotel, the Queen Anne. This hotel will be renovated in a second phase together with existing apartments in the same building, transforming these into 23 units. Conix Architects described this project as a 'journey within a journey'.

The starting point was a study of the possibilities and circumstances in a city like Brussels. Conix Architects realized that Brussels is undergoing a rejuvenating process thereby attracting a lot of young people. This new energy led them to various new themes. All aspects of 'meeting' were considered and chosen as the main theme. There are various instances of meeting or connecting such as nature and city, design and styles, sounds, music and dance, fashion, and the typical Brussels lifestyle. Conix Architects were guided by the spatial and social context of specific buildings such as Le Théâtre National, KVS, Kaaitheater, and Antoine Dansaert street with its well-known cafés, dance troupes, musicians, street artists and many more.

Getting to know all these elements is close to impossible especially for visitors, tourists or business people. However, Conix Architects want to reflect this journey in the hotel's design. The synergy of the city had to be tangible in the hotel's design and planning. The dialog between planning and the architectural design is expanded: the entrance will look like a catwalk, the bar like a cocktail lounge, the lobby like a retreat showing projections of modern day Brussels.

Conix Architects envisage 80 bedrooms, each with an area of 237 sq ft. Despite the compactness, they have found enough space to design a stylish and exclusive room. The rooms give a sense of spaciousness, partly due to their open-plan design and a see-through bathroom with glass partitions. In the same way, the window sill is extended to become part of the interior.

Hotel guests moving around as well as the abstract movement in a city were the main inspiration for designing the façade. This movement leads to exceptional confrontations similar to those when travelling and staying in hotels.

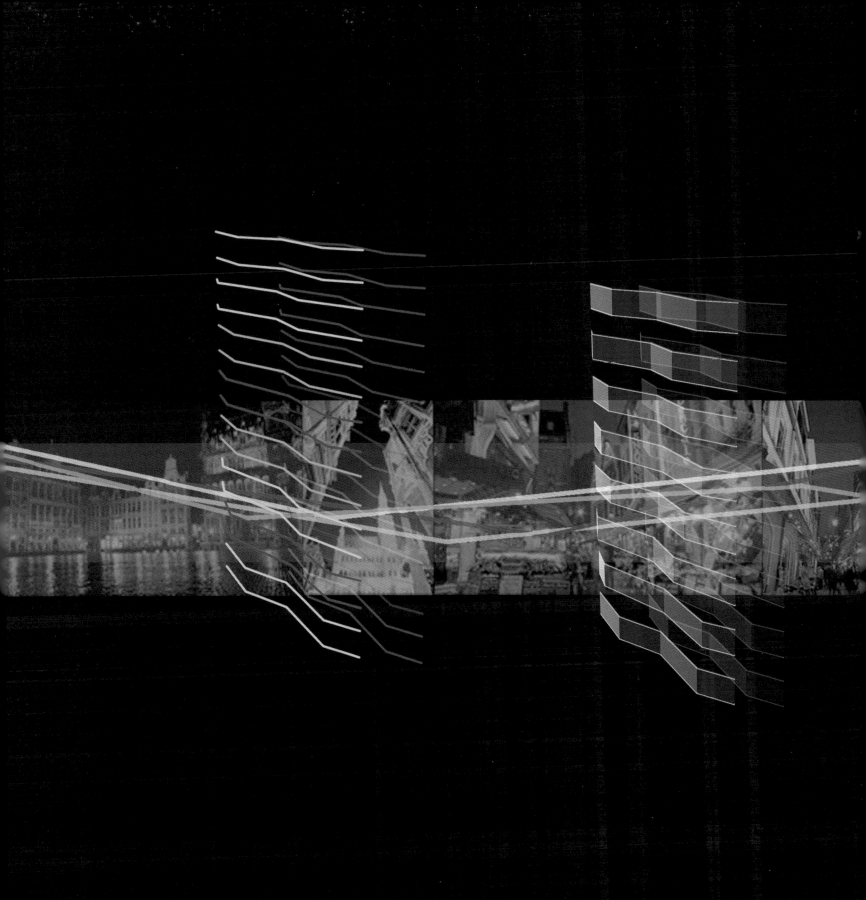

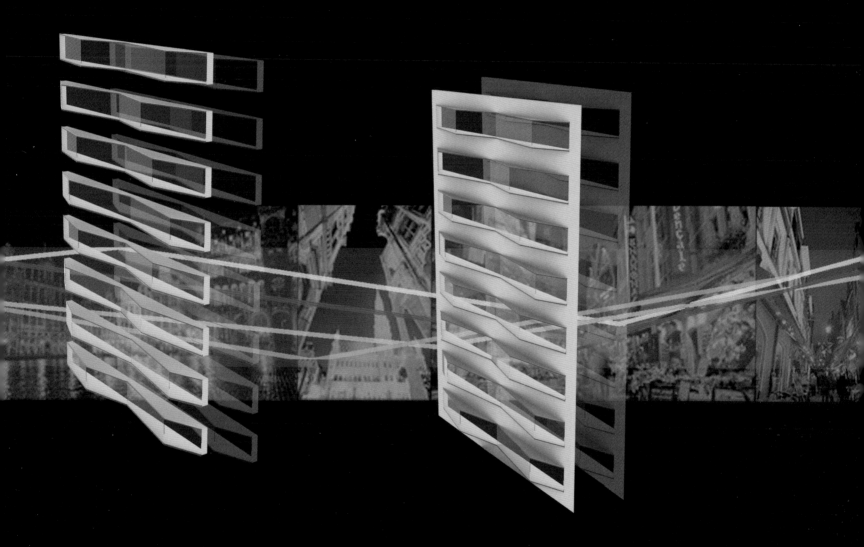

Client: Vooruitzicht nv – Date: 2004 – Area: 10.700 m² / 115,200 sq ft

Over the last 10 years, increased development of the suburb of Berchem on the outskirts of Antwerp has shaped the area. Offices as well as housing areas are being developed near the Berchemstadionstraat. The area near the Filip Williotstraat, called 'De Veldekens', was set aside for quality and affordable housing.

The area is divided into three project zones: A, B and C. Apartments will be developed in zones A and B, whereas C is earmarked for houses. At the corner where Filip Williotstraat and Berchemstadionstraat meet, the free-standing apartment block A signifies the start and the end of the house fronts. The street level is partly open to provide a view of the houses in zone C at the back. Sixty apartments will be built in zones A and B, divided into two blocks with 12 and 48 units, respectively. There will be a choice of one-, two- or three-bedroom apartments.

The main building's façade is flat with some cut-aways. Walled-in terraces and alternating cornice heights create a varied look. The cornice heights of the central part of the back wall are limited to four building layers to prevent the walls from impacting on the quality of light and views of those houses nearest to the building. As the apartment block faces towards the street, it also serves as a social control area. A strip of lawn in front of the building creates an open and spacious feeling but separates the public area from the private. On the one hand, block A forms the end of this zone, but on the other hand, it opens the way to the nearby houses. In this way, the area is clearly structured as to where one can walk. The passageway leads to a park that is nearly completely enclosed. As a result, the density diminishes gradually thereby connecting to the living area. The design for the apartment developed from a conceptual quest for variety within one building. The design process became a search for complexity and variety but based on a rational take on living. Within this rationally designed structure, Conix Architects were striving to find the right composition which would reflect a predominantly urban look. By adding passageways and lines of sight, this aspect was emphasized thereby creating an airy and clear construction.

Project zone C comprises of clusters of family houses. Conix Architects wanted to have variation on the theme but had to bear in mind what it would look like from the street too. In this neighborhood, they focused on every individual house. Playful design, varying cornice heights, different roof slopes and volume interaction between the different houses formed the spatial lines of force in this new prototype house. These garden homes are situated in a greenbelt. By making provision for a driveway, front gardens and more green areas on the street and at the back, this feature is further enhanced. There will be 30 houses in total, each unit with its own specific design and look, connected in a different way to the other units. To achieve this, three basic designs were made. Every house has four bedrooms, allowing for the optimum use of space for any type of family composition. This residential precinct is ideal for young families as it is close to the town center but still in a quiet, green area.

KANUNNIK PEETERSSTRAAT

FILIP WILLIOTSTRAAT

BERCHEMSTADIONSTRAAT

N

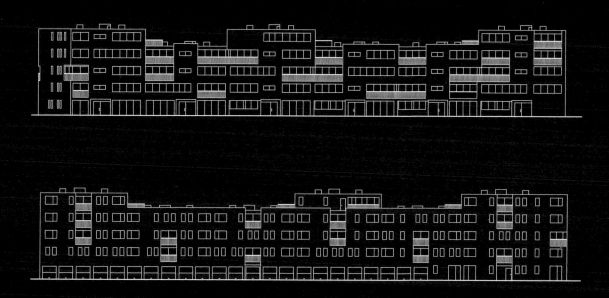

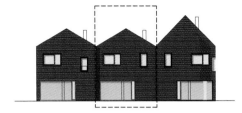

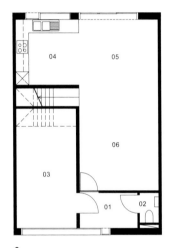

**0**

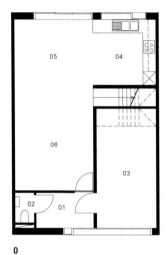

**0**

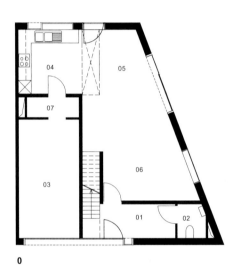

**0**

**1**

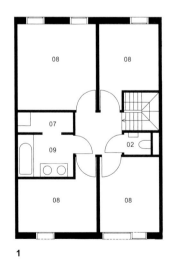

**1**

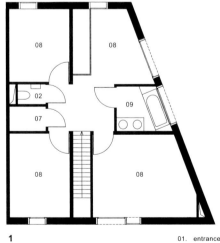

**1**

01. entrance
02. toilet
03. garage
04. kitchen
05. dining room
06. living room
07. storage
08. bedroom
09. bathroom

01. entrance
02. toilet
03. garage
04. kitchen
05. dining room
06. living room
07. storage
08. bedroom
09. bathroom

01. entrance
02. toilet
03. garage
04. kitchen
05. dining room
06. living room
07. storage
08. bedroom
09. bathroom

'God is in the details.' - LUDWIG MIES VAN DER ROHE

Christine Conix was born on 20 May 1955 in Lier, Belgium. She studied architecture at HAIR (*Higher Institute for Architecture*) in Antwerp, where she graduated with a Master's degree in 1978. Shortly afterwards, in 1979, she set up her own architectural firm, which became Architectenbureau Christine Conix bvba in 1989, of which she was Managing Director and main shareholder. In 2000, a different structure was chosen to ensure the office continuity. In this new structure a board of external advisors was created in order to broaden their vision. Furthermore, this structure also offered investment opportunities for creative and motivated collaborators who want to become partner.

The architectural firm has grown steadily over the years in terms of diversification, the extent of the projects, their size as well as in content. Winning competitions for more extensive projects in Brussels gave an even greater impulse to the growth. Consequently, the offices had to be enlarged to accommodate the growing international profile. During all these years their approach never changed: to deliver to clients creative and sustainable solutions combined with high quality design.

Sylvie Bruyninckx was born on the 10th of September 1972 in Louvain and studied architecture at the *University college of Science and Art, Dept. Architecture, Saint-Lucas*, where she obtained her Master degree in 1997. She started her international career at Mecanoo Architects in Delft (the Netherlands) and remained there for four years. Subsequently, she moved to London and worked for some years as a project architect at Erik van Egeraat Associated Architects. In 2003, she returned to Belgium and started working at Conix Architects in Antwerp. In January 2005, Sylvie Bruyninckx became a partner.

Today, the office is run by Christine Conix (Chief Executive Officer) and Sylvie Bruyninckx (Partner).
A staff of 67, working in the Brussels and Antwerp offices, form a steady base for the international opportunities.
Creative and motivated architects are offered the opportunity to join Conix Architects as partners in the future.

Ann Decock
Anne Dubois
An Steylaerts
Bert Stoffelen
Christine Conix
Colette Barré
Danny Cabuy
Filip Tack
Herman Remes
Ignace Pollentier
Jan Van Cleynenbreugel
Joep Debie
Johan Buelens
Karen Lansloot
Katia Goossens
Koen De Bock
Koen Van Grimbergen
Marianne Antonsen
Nathalie Mousny
Raf Van Tichelen
Sandra Symus
Stein Van Rossem
Ursula Pauwels
Veerle Moermans
Willem Walschap

An Steylaerts
Annemie Verbraeken
Benoît Jacques
Bert Stoffelen
Christian Burzer
Christine Conix
Colette Barré
Danny Cabuy
Dorothea W. Bos
Fabien Dautrebande
Filip Tack
Hadewijn Neirinck
Helga Spaey
Ignace Pollentier
Jan Van Cleynenbreugel
Jean-Marie Jans
Jeroen Theuns
Joep Debie
Johan Buelens
Karen Lansloot
Koen De Bock
Koen Van Grimbergen
Mark Janssen
Nathalie Mousny
Raf Van Tichelen
Rosalie Kim
Sandra Symus
Sophie Top
Tamara Vermeersch
Ursula Pauwels
Willem Walschap

Alexander Maes
Alexis Herbosch
An Steylaerts
Benoît Jacques
Bert Stoffelen
Christian Burzer
Christine Conix
Colette Barré
Danny Cabuy
Dat Schöffner
Debby Haepers
Dorothea W. Bos
Eveline Slijper
Evy Kinoo
Fabien Dautrebande
Filip Tack
Helga Spaey
Ignace Pollentier
Jan Van Cleynenbreugel
Jean-Marie Jans
Joep Debie
Johan Buelens
Jurgen Remmerie
Karen Lansloot
Koen Van Grimbergen
Koen Verhoeven
Mark Janssen
Michael van Impe
Nathalie Mousny
Raf Van Tichelen
Rosalie Kim
Sandra Symus
Sofie Van de Voorde
Ursula Pauwels
Willem Walschap

| 2003 | 2004 | 2005 | 2006 |
|------|------|------|------|
| Alexander Maes | Alexander Maes | Aldo Tornaghi | Aldo Tornaghi |
| An Luyten | An Luyten | Alexander Maes | Alissia Tassiopoulou |
| Ann Willekens | An Steylaerts | An Luyten | An De Dycker |
| An Steylaerts | Bart Mermans | An Steylaerts | An Steylaerts |
| Bart De Jong | Benoît Jacques | Barbara Roosen | Annemie Engels |
| Bart Wouters | Bert Stoffelen | Benoît Jacques | Barbara Roosen |
| Benoît Jacques | Caroline Gérard | Bert Nijs | Benoît Jacques |
| Bert Stoffelen | Caroline Pasmans | Bert Stoffelen | Caroline Gérard |
| Caroline Gérard | Celine de Wulf | Caroline Gérard | Christoph Thijs |
| Catherine Tuck | Christoph Thijs | Christoph Thijs | Christine Conix |
| Christine Conix | Chris Van Cammeren | Christine Conix | Christopher Renders |
| Debby Haepers | Christine Conix | Christopher Renders | Cindy Dreesen |
| Edward Sorgeloose | David Peeters | Cristian Crisan | Claire Fransen |
| Elke De Neef | David Rato | David Peeters | Cristian Crisan |
| Eveline Slijper | Dean Rikanovic | David Rato | David Peeters |
| Fabien Dautrebande | Debby Haepers | Dean Rikanovic | David Rato |
| Filip Tack | Dominique Fouchard | Dominique Delmarcelle | Dominique Delmarcelle |
| Inge Hegge | Edward Sorgeloose | Dominique Fouchard | Dominique Fouchard |
| Jan Van Cleynenbreugel | Ellen Smets | Edward Sorgeloose | Edward Sorgeloose |
| Jessica De Lannoy | Eve Deprez | Els Van Roy | Elena Kerdova |
| Joep Debie | Eveline Slijper | Emanuel Jonckx | Els Van Roy |
| Joeri Vangansbeke | Fabien Dautrebande | Fabien Dautrebande | Emanuel Jonckx |
| Karen Lansloot | Filip Tack | Filip Cleynen | Fabien Dautrebande |
| Karen Loyens | Jan Jespers | Gerda Boey | Filip Cleynen |
| Koen Van Grimbergen | Jessica De Lannoy | Gökce Cicek | Gilles Hasbroucq |
| Kris De Winter | Johan Nielsen | Gonzalo Vazquez | Gökce Cicek |
| Leen De Wilde | Julie Lagasse | Ilse Schrauwen | Gonzalo Vazquez |
| Marc Moutschen | Karen Loyens | Ingrid Manger | Hugues Couwenbergh |
| Marco De Lugnani | Kevin Charpentier | Jan Jespers | Ilse Schrauwen |
| Mark Janssen | Klare Bruyneel | Jessica De Lannoy | Ineke Verbruggen |
| Matthias Mattelaer | Koen Van Grimbergen | Johan Nielsen | Ingrid Manger |
| Nathalie Mousny | Kris De Winter | Johnny Fockenier | Jan Jespers |
| Olivier Salens | Laurien Pinxten | Joris Malbrain | Johan Nielsen |
| Pascal Storms | Leen De Wilde | Karen Loyens | Johnny Fockenier |
| Peter Nicolay | Manu Gelders | Kevin Charpentier | Joris Malbrain |
| Peter Sanders | Marc Moutschen | Klare Bruyneel | Jozef Hessel |
| Pierre Lemeire | Marco De Lugnani | Laurent Arnoldi | Karen Loyens |
| Pieter Tan | Mark Janssen | Laurien Pinxten | Karin Permeke |
| Raf Van Tichelen | Matthias Mattelaer | Leen De Wilde | Kevin Charpentier |
| Sandra Symus | Mira Gajić | Linda Cappetijn | Kirsti Bal |
| Sylvie Bruyninckx | Nathalie Seys | Mae Doms | Klare Bruyneel |
| Tanguy Oosterlynckx | Nicolas Coets | Manu Gelders | Laurent Arnoldi |
| Veerle Cools | Olivier Salens | Marc Biesmans | Leen Platevoet |
| Wendy Van den Wyngaert | Pedro Miguel Monteiro de Sousa | Marc Moutschen | Laurien Pinxten |
| | Peter Sanders | Marco De Lugnani | Linda Cappetijn |
| | Pieter Tan | Mark Janssen | Magdalena Kurzepa |
| | Raf Van Tichelen | Maya Einhaus | Malgorzata Idzikowska |
| | Sandra Symus | Mira Gajić | Manu Gelders |
| | Sylvie Bruyninckx | Monika Majdaniuk Krzesiak | Manu Gryson |
| | Titania Vandevelde | Nico Ivens | Matthias Van Rossen |
| | Wendy Van den Wyngaert | Nicolas Coets | Maya Einhaus |
| | Veerle Cools | Nicolas Schuybroek | Mich Wassinck |
| | Vincent Scohy | Olivier Salens | Migel Debakker |
| | Wouter Plessers | Ouafa Riani el Achab | Mira Gajić |
| | | Patricia Coppieters | Mohammed Hadouidi |
| | | Pedro Miguel Monteiro de Sousa | Nico Ivens |
| | | Peter Sanders | Nicolas Coets |
| | | Philippe Lemaître | Nicolas Schuybroek |
| | | Raf Van Tichelen | Ouafa Riani el Achab |
| | | Rina van Charante | Pedro Miguel Monteiro de Sousa |
| | | Sandra Symus | Peter Sanders |
| | | Sylvie Bruyninckx | Philippe Duren |
| | | Valerie Brasseur | Philippe Lemaître |
| | | Veerle Cools | Rebecca Gischer |
| | | Vincent Scohy | Rina van Charante |
| | | Wouter Plessers | Ruben Braeken |
| | | | Sebastiano Ghezzi |
| | | | Sophie Green |
| | | | Steven De Pauw |
| | | | Sylvie Bruyninckx |
| | | | Valerie Brasseur |
| | | | Vera Steuer |
| | | | Vincent Scohy |
| | | | Wim Crombez |
| | | | Wouter Plessers |

2005

ARCHITECTURE COMPETITION: THE 4ᵀᴴ EUROPEAN SCHOOL IN BRUSSELS

Nominated to design and execute complete technical studies for a school building. In collaboration with Archi 2000, Atelier du Sart Tilman, Duijsens and Meyer Viol, Marcq & Roba.
The team won the commission.

2004

ARCHITECTURE COMPETITION: THE ATOMIUM IN BRUSSELS

Design for renovating the six spheres and the ground floor. Conix Architects won the commission.

ARCHITECTURE COMPETITION: EAST FLANDERS PROVINCE

Extension of a multifunctional office building in Gouvernementstraat in Ghent. In conjunction with engineering bureau Provoost, Stockman and Mebumar.
Conix Architects won the commission.

INTERIOR COMPETITION: KAREL DE GROTE HOGESCHOOL

Interior design of ground floor of this college. Conix Architects won the commission

ARCHITECTURE COMPETITION: THE INTERNATIONAL SCHOOL IN EINDHOVEN (NL)

Nominated to design and execute complete technical studies for school building. In collaboration with Duijsens & Meyer Viol. The entire team was nominated to participate in the final round.

2003

INTERIOR COMPETITION SIBELGA

Interior design of an office building in Brussels. Conix Architects won the commission.

2002

ARCHITECTURE COMPETITION: ISVAG

Design for extending offices of incinerator in Wilrijk as well as a visitor's center. Conix Architects won the commission in collaboration with Arcade.

2000

ARCHITECTURE COMPETITION: VIB

New research building and technology park in Ghent. Conix Architects won the commission.

ARCHITECTURE COMPETITION: KAZERNE BLAIRON

Conversion of barracks to campus center in Turnhout. Conix Architects won the commission.

TOWN COUNCIL BOOM, PUT

New housing, in collaboration with the architecture firm Creabo. Conix Architects won the commission.

ARCHITECTURE COMPETITION: RAMEN GENT

Design of underground parking garage, houses and office building. Nominated to participate in final round.

ARCHITECTURE COMPETITION: SINT NIKLAAS

In collaboration with the architecture firm Buro 5, a town planning and architectural bureau in Maastricht. Design and urban development and architecture of the station in Sint Niklaas.
Nominated to participate in final round.

1998

ARCHITECTURE COMPETITION: COUNTY HALL FLEMISH BRABANT, LEUVEN

In collaboration with Poponcini & Lootens, Engineering architects. Nominated to participate in final round.

1996

ARCHITECTURE COMPETITION: GEMEENTEKREDIET, PROVINCIAL HEAD OFFICE, ANTWERP

Conix Architects won the commission.

1994

ARCHITECTURE COMPETITION: GENERALE BANK, BRANCH OFFICE, HEIST-OP-DEN-BERG

Conix Architects won the commission.

1993

ARCHITECTURE COMPETITION: GIMV

New office building in Antwerp. Conix Architects won the commission.


1990

ARCHITECTURE COMPETITION: PIME

Organized by County Board of Antwerp. Conix Architects won the commission.


1989

ARCHITECTURE COMPETITION:  COMPRIMO

Conversion of industrial hall into offices. Conix Architects won the commission.

ARCHITECTURE COMPETITION: 'SENIORIE'

Conversion of convent into retirement village in Lint. Conix Architects won the commission.


1983

ARCHITECTURE COMPETITION: AGFA GEVAERT

New office building in Mortsel. Conix Architects was nominated to participate in the final round.


**AWARDS**

2006

STAALBOUWWEDSTRIJD (STAALINFOCENTRUM)

Conix won the competition (architectural and esthetical follow-up of the project)

LENSVELT DE ARCHITECT INTERIEUR

Nomination for the interior renovation of Atomium.

LEAF (Leading European Architect Forum) AWARDS

Nomination for the interior renovation of Atomium.


2004

IF DESIGN AWARD 2004

Conix architects won the competition in collaboration with Enthoven Associates for the design of emergency lighting for ETAP.


1993

PRESS AWARD

'Cogels Osylei' house in Antwerp.

CONIX ARCHITECTEN, *Architectenbureau Christine Conix*. Nr. 1, Antwerp, 1999.

CONIX ARCHITECTEN, *Architectenbureau Christine Conix*. Nr. 2, Antwerp, 2001.

CONIX ARCHITECTEN, *Conix Architecten*. Nr. 3, Antwerp, 2003.

BERTIAU, WILLY. Woning als laboratorium, in *Financieel-economische tijd*, 5 July 2003.

BERTIAU, WILLY. Christine Conix ontwerpt hoofdzetel HNN, in *Financieel-economische tijd*, 5 July 2003, 15.

DE BRUYN, JOERI. Vernieuwd Atomium moet één miljoen bezoekers lokken, in *A+ Belgisch tijdschrift voor architectuur* n°194, June-July 2005, 10.

DIJK, PANCRAS. Nieuwe huid van roestvrij staal, in *National Geographic Nederland-België n° 2*, Diemen, 2003, 4-5.

DUPLAT, GUY. Kroniek van een restauratie, in *A+ Belgisch tijdschrift voor architectuur n° 198*, Brussels, 2006, 34-41.

EGGERICK, LAURE. In beeld - coup d'œil, Het ontvangstpaviljoen van het Atomium - Le pavillon d'accueil de l'Atomium, in *Staal / Acier n° 12*, Brussels, 2006, 16-17.

GOOSSENS, CAROLINE. Verfraaiing van een nationaal symbool, in *De Architect Interieur n° 20*, The Hague, 2006, 48-51.

HEIRMAN, FRANK. Rust in goede vorm, in *Gazet van Antwerpen*, November 2003, 14-17.

JENSEN, WILL. Christine Conix, in *Exclusief n° 145*, Antwerp, 2006, 72-80.

LANG, MARGARET. Atomium, Ideal Felt, Sibelga, Conti 7, Reynaers Aluminium, Bureaux Louise-Marie, Hesse Noord Natie, Blairon NV, ISVAG, Van den Berg, Creyf's Interim, KBC, Anselmo, Recticel, Himmos Put N, Kaïros McKinsey, Himmos Platinkaai, Himmos Upstream, GIMV, ETAP Lichtpaviljoen in Malle, in *Architecture & Urbanisme n° 8*, Brussels, 2006, 187-201.

MASSONI, GIOVANNA. Renovation of the Atomium in Belgium, in *Damn° Magazine n° 6*, Brussels, 2006, 80.

NAMIAS, OLIVIER. La Renaissance de l'Atomium, in *Archiescopie n° 59*, Paris, 2006, 16-17.

RICHARDSON, VICKY. Atomic Power, in *Blueprint*, London, 58-62.

SIOEN, LIEVEN. Een architect is geen artiest die een showke opvoert, in *De Morgen Magazine*, 13 November 2004, 26-31.

STADHOUDERS, ARJAN & MARJEL METTAU. Stralend staal vervangt mat aluminium, in *Gevelbouw n° 1*, Breda, 2006, 6-13.

STEINBERG, CLAUDIA. Restoring an icon of optimism, in *The New York Times*, 9. February 2006, New York.

SWIMBERGHE, PIET. Ze glimmen als nieuw, in *Knack Weekend*, October 2005, 184-189.

TILOT, CAROLIE & WIVINE DETRAUX. Atomium, Son histoire et sa rénovation/ haar geschiedenis en haar renovatie, in *L'Eventail*, 2006, 40-41-46-47-56-57.

VAN LIERDE, LUDWIG. Bouwen in Conixlijke stijl, in *Ondernemers*, March 2003, 50-54.

YODA, KANAE. Conix Architecten, Renovation, in *Architecture and Urbanism n° 432*, Tokyo, 2006, 90-93.

MORE PROJECTS

'Form follows function.' – LOUIS SULLIVAN

'Form becomes feeling.' – FRANK LLOYD WRIGHT

RECTICEL

IDEAL FELT

FORTIS COMMERCIAL
FINANCE

FERRANESI

HIMMOS BOECHOUT

HOUSE DZ

ETAP

HOUSE W

KAIROS-MCKINSEY

HOUSE VB

TOTAL FINA

EMBASSY TOKYO

OUSE O

PIME

DE POST MACHELEN

HOUSE R

HIMMOS PLANTIN

THALASSA

CASA VITAE

'KAZERNE BLAIRON'

REYNAERS ALUMINIUM

COGELS OSYLEI

HOUSE T

HIMMOS UPSTREAM

GIMV

OUSE M

KBC SCHILDE

COMPRIMO

ING LOUISE MARIE

DEXIA

CONSULATE OF THE
NETHERLANDS

HOUSE D

USG PEOPLE

UGC

233

INTERIOR

235

VISUALISATIONS

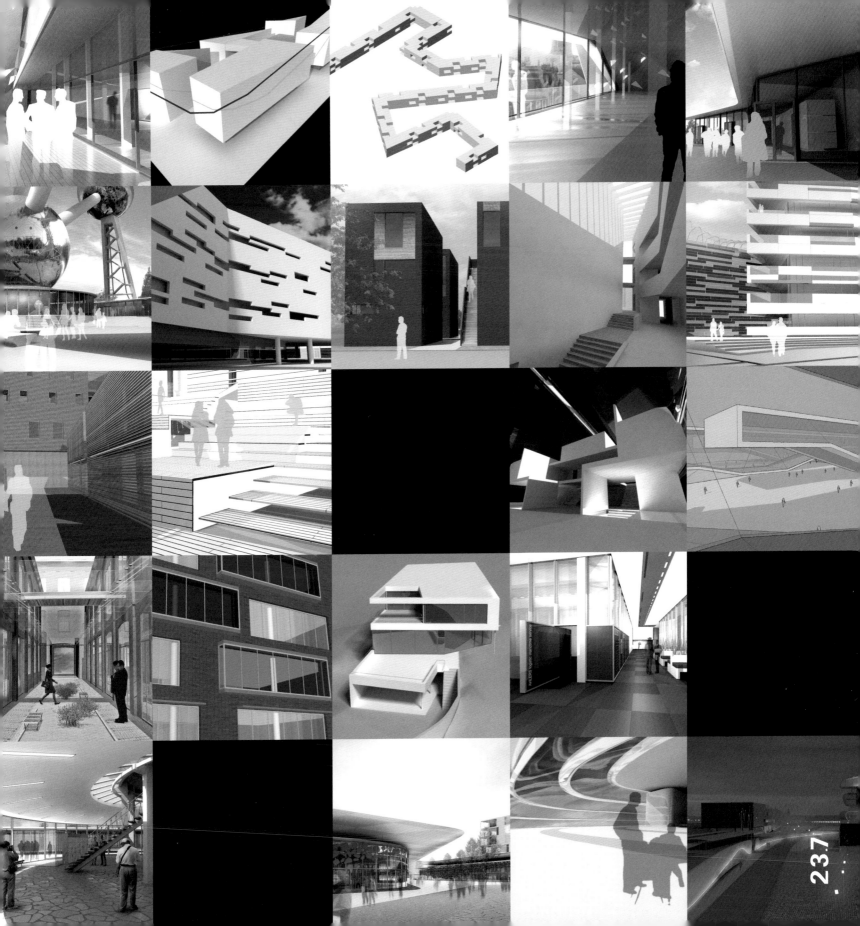

None of our projects could have been realized without the unrelenting trust of our clients, the dynamic team at Conix Architects, the inspirational solutions of our engineering partners, our contractors, our friends and family, and so many others who have always supported us and believed in us.

We would like to thank everyone who took part in the making of this book and everyone who has made a contribution to our work.

Wishing to create many more projects filled with emotions with and for you.

*Christine and Sylvie*

**CONIX ARCHITECTS cvba**
Cockerillkaai 18, B-2000 Antwerpen
tel +32(0)3 259 11 30   fax +32(0)3 259 11 49

Van Meyelstraat 30, B-1080 Brussel
tel +32(0)2 425 77 84   fax +32(0)2 425 78 20

www.conixarchitects.com   info@conixarchitects.com

TEXT

Kas Oosterhuis
Moniek E. Bucquoye
Conix Architects

PHOTOGRAPHY

| | | |
|---|---|---|
| Marie-Françoise Plissart | | 14-15 |
| Michel Vaerewijck | www.car-wash.net | 21 |
| Tom Vack | | 25 |
| Serge Brison | www.sergebrison.com | 3, 12-13, 26-27, 30, 33-35, 38, 64-65, 67, 69, 71, 72-75,77-80, 82-83, 102-105, 107-109, 111, 136-138, 157, 160-161, 163-167, 181, 184-185, 202-203, 205-206, 209, 217, 218-219 |
| Elisabeth Broekaert | www.elisabeth.broekaert.com | 96-99, 117, 154-155 |
| Anne-Mie Battheu | | 99,101 |
| Marc Detiffe | www.detiffe.com | 158-159 |
| Christophe Licoppe | www.licoppe.be | 118-119 |
| Wim Hendrix | | 218 |
| Caroline Monbailliu | www.monbi.be | 113-115 |

VISUALISATIONS

| | | |
|---|---|---|
| Philippe Steels | www.pixelab.be | 46-53, 56-57, 90-95, 127, 129, 140-142, 145, 194-199 |
| Pixyz | www.pixyz.be | 206 |
| Conix Architects | | 28-29, 55, 67, 70, 119-121, 123, 125, 129, 151-153, 169, 171-173, 183, 186-187, 189-191, 193, 196-197, 200-201 |

TRANSLATION

Ilze Raath

CONCEPT & LAYOUT

Conix Architects

PRINTED BY

Graphic Group Van Damme, Oostkamp (BE)

BINDING

Brepols Books & Bindery, Turnhout (BE)

PUBLISHED BY

Stichting Kunstboek bvba
Legeweg 165
B-8020 Oostkamp
tel  +32(0)50 46 19 10   fax +32 (0)50 46 19 18
www.stichtingkunstboek.com
info@stichtingkunstboek.com

ISBN 978-90-5856-217-3
D/2007/6407/01
NUR: 648